D1486282

COLLECTED POEMS
of
ELIZABETH DARYUSH

Elizabeth Daryush

COLLECTED POEMS

with an introduction by

DONALD DAVIE

Carcanet New Press

Acknowledgements are due to the editor of the *Southern Review* in which 'Air & Variations' was first published.

Verses: Seventh Book, with a Preface by Roy Fuller, was first published in 1971 by Carcanet Press. *Selected Poems: Verses I-VI* was first published in 1972 by Carcanet Press.

SBN 85635 120 2

First published 1976
by Carcanet New Press
in association with Carcanet Press Limited
330-332 Corn Exchange Buildings
Manchester M4 3BG

Printed in Great Britain
by Eyre & Spottiswoode Limited
at Grosvenor Press, Portsmouth

CONTENTS

INDEX OF FIRST LINES

6

THE POETRY OF ELIZABETH DARYUSH

by Donald Davie

When an unprejudiced literary history of our century comes to be written, our failure to recognize Elizabeth Daryush will be one of the most telling and lamentable charges that can be laid at our door. The cold silence that has prevailed about her work, through one decade after another, is so total that there can be no question of fixing the blame here or there, finding scapegoats. We are *all* at fault, in a way that points therefore to some really deep-seated frivolity, superficiality, cynicism through several generations of readers of English poetry.

Certainly, I cannot absolve myself. For it happens that I had the good fortune to stumble, while I was still young, on the writings of the one critic who *did* recognize the achievement of this poet, who tried not once but many times to force his contemporaries to confront the challenge of her work. I mean, the late Yvor Winters. And why, I now angrily ask myself, did I, who knew that I had been instructed by Winters time and again about the poetry of our time and the past, flinch from the responsibility that his championing of Mrs. Daryush laid upon me as upon others who listened to him — some of whom, incidentally, rose to the occasion as I didn't? I have given the answer: mere frivolousness, an anxiety not to be too far out of the fashion, above all a demand for quick returns upon a very small investment of time and attention. There can be no excuse.

In his *Primitivism and Decadence* (1937) Winters printed the poem, 'Still-life', from Mrs. Daryush's *The Last Man & Other Verses* (1936):

Through the open French window the warm sun
lights up the polished breakfast table, laid
round a bowl of crimson roses, for one —
a service of Worcester porcelain, arrayed
near it a melon, peaches, figs, small hot
rolls in a napkin, fairy rack of toast,
butter in ice, high silver coffee-pot,
and, heaped on a silver salver, the morning's post.

She comes over the lawn, the young heiress,
from her early walk in her garden-wood,
feeling that life's a table set to bless
her delicate desires with all that's good,
that even the unopened future lies
like a love-letter, full of sweet surprise.

When Winters included *Primitivism and Decadence* as part
of his *In Defense of Reason* (1947), there was the Daryush
poem again. It was there that I read it first, and I kick my-
self for not having been incited by it, by something so
wholly unlike any other English poem of our time up to
that date. (Since then, Thom Gunn's 'Autumn Chapter in
a Novel', a poem which may owe something to 'Still-Life',
may be set beside it.) My excuse, a poor one, must be that
Winters cited and discussed the poem exclusively in relation
to its metre, as a fine example of what could be achieved
in English in a strictly *syllabic* metre, as distinct from the
more orthodox accentual-syllabic. A far more generally
illuminating discussion of the poem is in Winters's essay,
'Robert Bridges and Elizabeth Daryush' (in the *American
Review* for 1936-37). In this essay, which only the devoted
enterprise of Francis Murphy has made generally available,[1]
Winters wrote:

If we regard the subject-matter of this poem, we find

something rather curious: the matter explicitly described implies, largely through the ominous and melancholy tone, a social context which is nowhere mentioned, yet from which the poem draws its power, a power which is not only real but great. This implication probably reaches its most intense impression in the two lines, unforgettable in the melancholy of their cadence, which open the sestet; but was never absent.

And he goes on to relate this to a new element in what were in 1937 'the last two books' by Mrs. Daryush; that is to say, *Verses, Fourth Book* (1934) and *The Last Man & Other Verses* (1936). The new element Winters defines by saying: 'she appears to be increasingly conscious . . . of social injustice, of the mass of human suffering'. And this brings to our attention a matter of the first importance: Elizabeth Daryush, unlike her father Robert Bridges and unlike a greater poet of whom she sometimes reminds us, Thomas Hardy, is a poet in whom we can discern a development, not merely technical but thematic also, a deepening and changing attitude to the world she lives in. Quite simply, she has not lived through the first three quarters of the twentieth century in England without registering and responding to the profound changes that have transformed the world of the English gentry which, as the daughter of Robert Bridges, she was born to. No one is yet in a position to trace this development, and for the merest bare bones of it we are once again indebted to the one serious reader she had, Yvor Winters, who read her in California and never once in his life visited England: 'Mrs. Daryush has disowned her first three books, published in 1911, 1916, and 1921 and wishes them destroyed. . . . Her mature career may be said to have begun with *Verses*, published in 1930, to have reached its most perfect achievement in

Verses, Third Book, published in 1933, to have reached a crisis and collapse of form in *Verses, Fourth Book*, published in 1934, as a result, it would seem, of the discovery of new matter to which she found her style ill-adapted, and to have begun the mastery of this new matter, or of a few aspects of it, in *The Last Man & Other Poems*, published in 1936.' It would be odd if the nearly 40 years that have supervened since Winters wrote thus — years that have seen Mrs. Daryush continue writing up to *Verses: Seventh Book* (Carcanet Press, 1971) — do not cause us to revise, as well as extend, this account of her development. Meanwhile, however, Winters's comment is very much to the point: 'Her talent, then, although it was obviously formed by her father's influence, appears to have borne fruit only after his death, and to have developed very rapidly within a very short period, after a long period of stagnation.' And this is a good point at which to take note of the poem, 'Fresh Spring, in whose deep woods I sought', from *Verses, Third Book*, one of the Daryush poems which Winters most esteemed, which he learned with dismay that the author intended to suppress. I give it as my hesitant opinion that she was more nearly right about this, than he was.

For understandable reasons, not only Yvor Winters's account of Elizabeth Daryush but also the more belated and yet more momentous account of her by Roy Fuller, when he was Professor of Poetry at Oxford, gave disproportionate emphasis to her experiments with syllabics. If on the contrary we attend to the substance of 'Still-Life', to what it is saying, we shall find its companion-piece in 'Children of Wealth' which, originally in *Verses, Sixth Book*, appears only one poem away from 'Still-Life' in the *Selected Poems* which Elizabeth Daryush arranged for Carcanet Press in 1972. And 'Children of Wealth' is a sonnet in orthodox accentual-syllabics:

Children of wealth in your warm nursery,
Set in the cushioned window-seat to watch
The volleying snow, guarded invisibly
By the clear double pane through which no touch
Untimely penetrates, you cannot tell
What winter means; its cruel truths to you
Are only sound and sight; your citadel
Is safe from feeling, and from knowledge too.

Go down, go out to elemental wrong,
Waste your too round limbs, tan your skin too white;
The glass of comfort, ignorance, seems strong
To-day, and yet perhaps this very night

You'll wake to horror's wrecking fire — your home
Is wired within for this, in every room.

Each reader must decide for himself which of the metres —
syllabic, or accentual-syllabic — supplies him with the more
haunting, more memorably poignant, cadence. What cannot
be doubted is that the two poems support each other,
to show that the poet in the late 1930s came quite sudden-
ly to the perception of what her relatively privileged birth
committed her to, or excluded her from; the double pane
of glass which that privilege of birth erected between her
and the mass of suffering humankind. The perhaps excess-
ive, certainly very violent, pressures that disturb the penta-
meter in line 10 — 'Waste your too round limbs, tan your
skin too white' — indicate the desperation, barely under
control, with which the poet thus recognized and diagnosed
her plight. And as for the syllabics of 'Still-Life', since in
most readers' ears they are indistinguishable from free
verse, the gauntlet that Yvor Winters threw down in 1937
still lies where he cast it: 'One imagines that the medium

could not be used with greater beauty than in this poem; there is certainly nothing in the work of the American masters of free verse to surpass it, and there is little to equal it.' As much might be claimed, I'd say, for 'Forbidden Love' from *Verses, Fourth Book*, which is remarkable as perhaps the last thoroughly accomplished poem in English to invoke, with pride and without qualification, the chivalric code for the ordering of sexual relations. (Its language is accordingly, and quite properly, stilted.)

But it is more important to recognize that the poet's experiments with syllabics never stopped her from writing in more orthodox metres, nor is she manifestly better in the one sort of metre than the other. We've seen this already with the companion-pieces, 'Still-Life' and 'Children of Wealth'. A similar set of twins is 'Winter Larches', from *The Last Man*, and 'Here, where the larks sing, and the sun's so warm', from *Verses, Fourth Book*. Because these are what used to be called 'nature-poems', they are of course less intense than the poems we've looked at first. But as Wordsworth said, 'The human mind is capable of being excited without the application of gross and violent stimulants.' It's a saying which is relevant to many poems by Elizabeth Daryush, and not just to her 'nature-poems', numerous and lovely as those are.

In his own way Winters too asked for *intensity*. And that explains the praise that he heaped on 'Anger lay by me', from *The Last Man*:

> Anger lay by me all night long,
>   His breath was hot upon my brow,
> He told me of my burning wrong,
>   All night he talked and would not go.
>
> He stood by me all through the day,
>   Struck from my hand the book, the pen;

18

He said: 'Hear first what *I've* to say,
    And sing, if you've a heart to, *then*.'

And can I cast him from my couch?
    And can I lock him from my room?
Ah no, his honest words are such
    That he's my true-lord, and my doom.

Winters says of this, 'Such work represents, I believe, and in spite of the italics, which could easily . . . be dispensed with, the perfection of English poetic style . . .'; and also, 'There is much other great poetry in English, but poetry of this type, at its best, is probably the greatest, and in its purity of style and richness of meaning it defines the norm, the more or less clear consciousness of which probably gives much of their identity to the variant types'. To understand this, one needs to study Winters's criticism as a whole, and also his own poems; for it was his single-minded purpose through more than thirty years to restore poetry of this kind to the central place from which 19th-century and 20th-century opinion had dislodged it, with (as Winters saw the matter) disastrous results. Readers who have not had the benefit of Winters's instruction will almost certainly be baffled by the high claims he makes for a poem like this, so bare and seemingly so rigid. Such writing flies so directly in the face of current preconceptions about poetry that one does not come to love and admire it at all soon, or at all easily. A useful starting-point is Winters's confession: 'The quality which I personally admire most profoundly . . . is the ability to imbue a simple expository statement of a complex theme with a rich association of feeling, yet with an utterly pure and unmannered style.' Serviceable short cuts to what Winters is getting at might be afforded by some of the early poems of William Blake, and by (in

19

Blake's background) the best of the congregational hymns of the English 18th century — by Isaac Watts, Charles Wesley, and Cowper. And another way to get at the austere virtues of this style is to see them tightened into the fierce hostility of the epigram, as in this poem from *Verses, Fourth Book*:

> It is pleasant to hang out
> this sign at your open gate:
> 'Succour for the desolate' —
> your neighbours praise you, no doubt;
>
> but woe to whoe'er in need
> at the inner door has knocked,
> found the snug room barred and locked
> where alone you fatly feed.

And we may well think that this caustic image of the professional do-gooder brings us back to the social consciousness of 'Still-Life' and 'Children of Wealth'.

*　　　　*　　　　*

To have the poet-laureate for one's father is a grievous disadvantage for any poet to labour under. And there can be no doubt that the shadow which has eclipsed Elizabeth Daryush is the shadow of Robert Bridges. This is complicated by the fact that for the most part we have an inadequate and distorted idea of Robert Bridges, remembering him above all as the author of the unreadable *Testament of Beauty* and as the man who withheld from us, for longer than we think necessary, the poems of Gerard Manley Hopkins. We do not remember for instance that Bridges esteemed Ezra Pound, and was esteemed by him. And it should go without saying that Bridges, the author of 'Low Barometer' and 'A Passerby', is now and has been for many years a poet grotesquely under-rated. But what has brought this about (in so far as it isn't merely the lax and heartless turn of fashion) is something that it's quite easy to put our finger on; it is Bridges's *diction*, his choice of vocabulary. Pound put his finger on it, in the *Pisan Canto* 80:

> 'forloyn' said Mr. Bridges (Robert)
> 'we'll get 'em all back'
> meaning archaic words . . .

Diction is what puts us off in reading Bridges, and it is also, though not to the same degree, the great difficulty that we are likely to have with Elizabeth Daryush. Here, Winters will not help us. For diction was one dimension of poetry which Winters, so splendidly alert to other dimensions like above all metre and cadence, was rather consistently deaf to, and obtuse about. For instance, in his essay on Bridges and Daryush, he quotes, as an example of Bridges at his best, 'The Affliction of Richard', which contains the lines:

> But what the heavenly key,
> What marvel in me wrought
> Shall quite exculpate thee,
> I have no shadow of thought.

And Winters is quite unperturbed by — does not even notice — the utterly slack, unrealized and unrealizable metaphor in *'shadow* of thought'. To say that the language of these lines is what neither Bridges himself nor anyone else would in any conceivable circumstances ever *say* — this is a criticism of another sort, and one which, if pushed at all

21

far, lands us in absurdities. Nevertheless, it undoubtedly has its force. And we may as well concede that a diligent inquisition of Mrs. Daryush's poems would come up with passages against which these charges lie just as heavily as against these verses by her father.

On the other hand, if Winters pays too little attention to diction, other readers of our time — especially British ones — have concentrated on it to the virtual exclusion of all else. And this is probably a worse fault. One may make the admittedly hazardous suggestion that in all poetry except the greatest there has to be a sort of 'trade off' — of cadence as against diction, of diction as against cadence. And in that case what needs to be said is that, whereas with other poets we agree to buy a racy or pungent turn of speech at the cost of an ugly cadence (a bargain we are disconcertingly too ready to strike), in the case of Mrs. Daryush the trade-off is usually the other way round: we are required to tolerate a 'timeless' or archaic or improperly marmoreal expression for the sake of the beautiful and meaningful cadence which it makes possible. (This is not to deny that there are places where the game is not worth the candle, where the proffered bargain must be refused.)

But there is a stronger and better case that can be made for the use of such 'poetical' diction as is customary with Mrs. Daryush. And this rests on linking her, not with Bridges, but with the greater poet, Thomas Hardy. In the unwontedly elaborate and ode-like poem, 'The Waterfall', from *Verses, Sixth Book* (1938; it will be noted that her austerity extends to the titling of her books as well as the writing of them), we read:

A thousand feet of torn stream falling sheer
In fog and thunder . . . Like a theatre
The rocks had taken curve as, year by year,

> The torrent wore at its hard doom-way, inch by inch . . .
>   Imagination flew up, then would flinch
>   From looking down — hung dizzied, even here . . .

And who, that has read in the poetry of Thomas Hardy, would deny the epithet 'Hardyesque' to 'its hard doom-way'? Can we imagine Hardy ever *saying* those words, in conversation? And if we cannot, what does it matter? They are entirely in keeping with what we recognize as Hardy's characteristic idiom. And however bizarre we find that idiom when we first encounter it, however heterogeneous and unaccountable, we recognize it — as we go on reading Hardy's poems — as a universe of language which is self-consistent within its own self-chosen boundaries, allowing certain liberties and denying itself others. It is in this sense that every poet — except, once again, the very greatest — creates his own language within the language that we share with him, a distinctive language which is private only in the first place, which becomes steadily more public and available to us, the more we familiarize ourselves with it. To speak for myself, that process for good or ill works itself out in reading Elizabeth Daryush's poems as in reading Hardy's. And this, it will be observed, is an argument for not picking out the plums from the cake but on the contrary for presenting this poet's work in bulk and *in toto*.

Note
1. *Yvor Winters: Uncollected Essays and Reviews*, edited and introduced by Francis Murphy, Chicago, 1973.

NOTE ON SYLLABIC METRES

Some of the poems here re-printed are written on a syllabic system, and I should like to comment on what seems to be a wide-spread misunderstanding and under-estimate of what the principle implies: a strict syllable-count, although of course essential, is, in my view, merely the lifeless shell of its more vital requirements.

Accepting that not only a work of art but every aspect of its medium is intrinsically a contrived relation between the known and the uncomprehended, the fixed and the unpredictable, recalling, too, that in accentual verse, as in barred music, the fixed element is that of time, and the unfixed that of number (of syllables or notes) we can assess what part should be played by these factors in a truly syllabic system. Here the position is reversed: the fixed element is no longer time but number; the integrity of line and syllable is challenged by the stress-demands of sense or syntax. The aim of the artist will be so to balance these incommensurables as to reflect his own predicament of thought or feeling, thereby enhancing his consciousness of an imagined relation with the unattainable. The rules for achieving this are by their very nature unwritten ones, but a few guide-lines can be laid down.

In general, meaning should make the greatest possible use of time-variety without losing sight of the number-pattern. First, therefore, the line-ending, the highest point of emphasis and tension, being no longer led up to by steps of regular stress, must be established and maintained by other means. The first few lines of a syllabic poem should when possible be complete sentences or phrases. Rhyme is almost indispensable, but since it can be unaccented need be neither over-obvious nor monotonous. The integrity of the syllable must be ensured by the avoidance of all dubious elisions. Stress-variations are more effective in fairly short lines, and more easily obtained from those with an odd syllable-count, since here there is a choice of two equally accessible stress-counts. Full advantage should of course be taken of the release from stress-restrictions, with their often unavoidable distortions of the natural speech-rhythm. Inversions should now be used only for meaningful emphasis.

With these main principles in mind, the writer replaces the usual regular stress-waves by such other currents and cross-currents, such expectations and disappointments, as may further his purpose. He may, for instance, introduce the same irregularities into the corresponding lines of a lyric's every stanza; or he may repeat, often with great effect, in the last line of a poem, some startling upheaval in the first; or, again, he may use a similar break in a previously established pattern to express some violent change of mood or thought. These and many similar devices will with practice become the instinctively chosen instruments of the poet whose ear is attuned to their possibilities.

Without them, there will be no poem.

E. D.

SELECTED POEMS
VERSES I-VI

I made this garden, this heav'n of sight,
said the artist, I planned every bed
of beauty-hues, of fadeless delight.

I raised these woods, the musician said,
these lofty strains; I turned the bare ground
to groves celestial of noble sound.

But he whose paints are only rich words,
his tunes but twining thoughts, said: These grew,
these vines, I see not how, though upwards

I trained or pruned them as best I knew;
where gladness shone, where sorrow's stream flowed,
I found them, and beside the worn road.

Life, a tree of toil I plant thee;
Only thus to grow I'll grant thee:

Wax in sombre strength, devouring
All my plots of pleasant flowering:

Soar in resolution, slaying
All my lawns of small displaying:

Branch in ardour self-transcending:
Surpass even thy stern intending:

From thy root if nothing shake thee,
Then, though Time the woodman break thee,
He'll for beauty's building take thee.

Now the beauteous lamps are low:
Who'll stand forth, fair light to show?
I will, said the voice I know.

Who'll be for benighted man
A torch in his army's van?
I will, said he, *for I can*.

Who can his whole being fill
With fire, till that fire him kill?
I, said he, *if God so will*.

3
Rainbow at Dawn

Before the grey world was awake the arch of bliss
Was lit for me alone—not the wide arch of noon,
Low for the crowd's low stature—though now narrowing this
Swelled to a crescent zenith-high . . . gem-set it shone . . .
Lost in the plain's rain were the leaning plinths that held
The partly mastered ring that so my sight compelled.

And yet, the imperfection . . . Shall they never meet,
Those reaching arms, those beams of rain-translated light?
Shall not at last some magic morning clasp, complete
Glory's earth-image? . . . Though I climb my sombre height,
Though I may glimpse before the dawn my mirrored sun,
With day the haunting vision is undone . . . undone . . .

4

Full filled with happiness, yet knowing not
To whom my brimming heart should bear its praise,
Afire with strength, yet uninformed to what
To dedicate my soaring powers' assays,
Drinking the water sweet that's my sweet lot,
Warmed at all-warming youth's triumphal blaze,
All have I, save the clue to this thought's knot:
Whither and whence are drawn my wondrous days?

Ah, how could thus the stream of gladness flow
If fed not from some height's eternal spring?
Ah, what could fire ascending ardour so
But ardour's very sun, but life's own king?
And to what end, if not that I may know
Joy, zeal increased, under his ordering?

5
Persian Dawn

The air is light; the rustling leaves
    Of the tall planes remember not
Nor the loud jays, how yestereve's
    Oppression hung, a burden hot:

The village street knows naught amiss,
    The chattering workers go their ways,
As though they too forgot how this
    Morn also must, with mounting blaze

Through steep laborious heats lead on
    To noon's rock-summit of distress,
To the grim path whose goal is won,
    At last, of night, of pathlessness.

I prayed that on my mortal road
   Endless truth would enlighten me;
The gloom said: 'What is this thy God,
   To thus attend and answer thee?'

I said: 'The brightest that I know,
   My warmest thought, to this I kneel:
To this in ecstasy I bow,
   To this in anguish I appeal.'

The sun rose up in glory strong
   And said: 'Behold my heavenly blaze:
'Tis I alone to whom belong
   Thy dawns, thy now so lustrous days:

''Twas I who from brute mire thy spark
   Created, fanned, till up it strove;
'Twas I who in thy terror dark
   Lit for thee faith and hope and love:

''Twas I alone who, lulling thee,
   In rhythms did thy life arrange,
Who then to thought continually
   Quickened thee with the varying change

'Of hour and month and season fair' —
   I murmured: 'Yes; and yet, I know
That past this warmly pulsing sphere
   Surges infinity's cold flow

'Of forces that no flesh can chart,
   Where life, if any life there be,
Is alien to my human heart,
   Is naught that can companion me;

'I know that in that ocean blent
   Of time with triple-brinkéd space,
All the primeval firmament
   Is but a point, an instant's place,

'A fleck of foam that in some thrall
   Is gripped a moment and is gone —
A droplet is the earth, and all
   The lucent film of life thereon,

'A mote that through some mighty beam
   Of stress is drawn, and thus is lit
To life, to love, that so must seem
   To us the force that fashioned it,

'For we, the breakings of that strain
   In the unknown, are not till dim power's
O'ercharge — its urge of lifeless pain
   Ends in the pain-flash that is ours,

'In lightnings fierce of passionate need,
   Of eager giving . . . When again
Shall vivid wish and word and deed
   Vanish, burnt out, what then, what then? . . .'

The rocket of man's reaching thought
   Soars, soars, then quivers, pauses, breaks
In coloured stars: the mind distraught
   In fading sparks, in art-fire speaks.

7
After Bank Holiday

Now deserted are the roads
   Where awhile the lovers went;
Vacant are the field-abodes
   Where a vivid hour they spent:
      Solemn dark
   Broods again in lane and park.

'Tis no matter where are gone
   Those warm lives — to halls, maybe,
Festive, or to lodgings lone:
   Of the land their tenancy
      Now is o'er;
   Earth to earth belongs once more.

Gone are they as hourly goes
   From the sombre fields of space
Our world, with its little glows —
   Passion's ship that has no place,
      Leaves no track,
   On time's endless ocean black.

Mortality, and her drear daughter, Age —
Mortality, that holds my joy's brief book,
Presenting slowly every ordered page,
Then turning it, ere I enough can look;
Stern-meting Age, filler of pleasure's glass,
Who ever subtler, paler wine must pour,
Richer, maybe, but, as the swift years pass,
Ever less sweet, till used be all my store —

O, there's no glory in the glowing day,
No splendour in the shining night, but she
Will whisper: 'This is passing soon for aye';
Or she: 'I'll give no more this ecstasy.'

'Crush I for ever now this leaf.' 'This flask
I break: for this again thou shalt not ask.'

9
Invalid Dawn

Above the grey down
    gather, wan, the glows;
relieved by leaden
    gleams a star-gang goes;

in the dark valley
    here and there enters
a spark, laggardly,
    to the faint watchers

that were there all night —
    factory, station
and hospital light . . .
    Tired of lamp, star, sun,

bound to my strait bed
    uncurtained, I see
heaven itself law-led,
    earth in slavery.

Once more
The sea of winter breaks upon a waveless shore;
I hear a sound
Of rippling (as of bird-song) over sunny ground;

Again
The tide of icy darkness, of starvation-bane,
Has turned to bring
Our ship to the warm cliffs (like orchards white) of spring,

Where soon
The mariners will land, as they have often done,
Whistling the while,
Impatient to explore another summer-isle,

To know
This one, too, of the endless archipelago —
Gladly, once more,
Have they forgot their charter, with its term obscure.

Seeing the company of Spring I say:
O, would that my words could command alway
The fair ones camping in my field today!

Would that I might, when meets she wintry doom,
Call back full-bosomed chestnut, to resume
Her billowy green frock worked with pearly bloom;

Would that I might be summoner of the charms
Of scented may, what time no more she warms
Out-holding to the sun her long white arms,

And lilac heavy-headed, drunk with all
Her fragrant dreaming, and laburnum tall
With her loose amber locks poetical,

And rhododendron, and her sister sweet
Luxurious azalea — where they meet
From gold to carmine is the flame complete,

And curly-headed hyacinth, and vain
Narcissus like a slim boy, in the train
Of amazonian tulip, smartly plain —

Would that I might, glad with immortal skill,
Set here for aye all who awhile now fill
My garden, followers of time's sad will!

The Poet and His Seasons

I have a pact with palmy spring:
Sweet happiness of whom I sing
Shall sing of me eternally.

I have a sign from summer proud:
The glory that I've chanted loud
Shall of my fame the furtherer be.

I have an oath from autumn drear:
Grief that I've mourned for shall endear
To all mankind my memory.

I have a word from wintry bane —
Most mighty terror, thou'lt remain
My monument, who mov'd'st not me.

Autumn, dark wanderer halted here once more,
Grave roamer camped again in our light wood,
With garments ragg'd, but rich and gorgeous-hued,
With the same fraying splendours as before —
Autumn, wan soothsayer, worn gipsy wise,
With melancholy look, but bearing bold,
With lean hard limbs careless of warmth or cold,
With dusky face, and gloomed defiant eyes,

You glanced at summer, and she hung her head;
You gazed, and her fresh cheek with fever burned;
You sighed, and from her flowery vales she turned;
You whispered, and from her fond home she fled:

Now seated by your tattered tent she broods
On timeless heights, eternal solitudes.

14
Song: Throw Away the Flowers

Throw away the flowers,
   they are no use,
   the faery bowers
of the former truce;
     fancy quickly dies
     under fear's dark skies.

Throw away the flowers,
   fetch stubborn rock;
   build for the hours
of terror and shock;
     go to timeless fact
     for what beauty lacked.

Throw away the flowers,
   the tender songs;
   attune your powers
to eternal wrongs;
     have but hopeless, hard
     rebellion for bard.

15
November Sun

His face is pale and shrunk, his shining hair
    Is prison-shorn;
Trailing his grey cloak, up the short dark stair
    He creeps each morn,

Looks out to his lost throne, to the noon-height
    Once his, then turns
Back to the alien dungeon, where all night
    Unseen he burns.

Anger lay by me all night long,
   His breath was hot upon my brow,
He told me of my burning wrong,
   All night he talked and would not go.

He stood by me all through the day,
   Struck from my hand the book, the pen;
He said: 'Hear first what *I've* to say,
   And sing, if you've the heart to, *then*.'

And can I cast him from my couch?
   And can I lock him from my room?
Ah no, his honest words are such
   That he's my true-lord, and my doom.

I am your lover now, once awful Enmity,
Once strange and gloomy Hate, now I your glory know;
You who erewhile were hell incarnate, now to me
Are heaven, the good for which all others I'll forgo —
    Now in imagination that I watch you wreak
     On your own folk the fires that they lit for the weak.

Mildness is no more, Tolerance is done to death,
Pity is buried deep, even Pardon is shut down
Among the shadows, starved of all but ghostly breath;
You alone live, their slaughterer grim, now lovely grown;
    Now could I die for you, who in mad dream I see
     Reversed on your own fiends, O now right enmity!

(After a massacre)

Thou say'st: *The clear stream is a troubled river grown* . . .
Would'st then confine it to one field's level alone?

Thou say'st: *The flowery sward is ploughed and heaped
                                    with stone* . . .
Would'st then the tree'd garden's high perfection postpone?

Thou say'st: *The hard woman doth the maiden dethrone* . . .
Would'st rank, O mortal, what's but to heaven's ruler known?

What I can's a voice,
kindly, musical,
saying: 'Rest, rejoice';

what I cannot, blares
like a trumpet-call
its rousing despairs.

What I can's a flower,
a lush leafy shoot,
very Eden's bower;

what I cannot, glows
like forbidden fruit,
whose wine-juice none knows.

20
Lullaby

Loose the horses now
from harness and plough,
let them plod off, slow,
head bent, stumblingly,
too tired out to see,
to the stall they know.

Follow them not there,
let them lie alone,
they'll be in the care
of a kind mistress,
she knows how to dress
bruiséd flesh and bone,

her simples are good
for soreness and ache,
at dawn they'll be back,
champing, lusty-thewed —
loose the horses now
from harness and plough.

Sleepless

'Tis for you to shut the door
of your room against the roar
of sorrow's on-thundering sea;

'tis for you to draw your blown
curtains close before the moon
of beauty that cannot be,

'tis for you to dout the fire,
to stamp on flickering desire . . .
In silence, obscurity,

'tis then for your Mother kind
to bring you the draught, to blind
and deafen your weary mind —
she will come; constant is she.

One creature, foul or fair,
What is't for Nature's care?
Her world of want and strife
Teems with contented life.

One spark, or low or higher,
What is't to the whole fire
Of human discontent,
Of lust malevolent?

Yet sainthood beckons thee . . .
Perish, then, speck apart
From man's fierce-flaming heart;
Die, white bird blown to sea
From earth's sufficiency.

March 21

The wood's alive today —
   Warm power all round
Breathes like a beast of prey
   Waiting to bound . . .

It was no timid bird,
   No harmless snake,
That rustle that I heard
   In the birch-brake;

It was no fair red bud
   On the larch-bough
That I saw, but drawn blood —
   The warning now

Of bliss that will not bide,
   Of need too full,
Too fierce, to be denied,
   Wild, terrible . . .

I am your mother, your mother's mother,
I am your father, his father also;
look on me, see each living ancestor;
it is well you should understand your kin,
should learn who your body's bound to, should know
who they are whose house you are prisoned in.

I am your dear spouse, your wife, your husband,
I am nearer to you than your own folk,
I am what you loved, freely chose, the friend
you cannot leave — ev'n in the tomb I wait
to be your soul's only companion . . . Look,
if you dare, on your mind's eternal mate.

(After Jalāl ud Din Rūmi)

    'Only relief, no less,
   Real flesh-relief, no false sublimation . . .'
To you who clamour thus, quick hour of temptation,
      Comes a dumb ghost;
  A sister-hour unshriven from the soul's own past
   Says with her gaze: 'Ah yes,

      I know, I know,
  Who once as you suffered, burned with thirst-woe;
   I am Persephone,
The sometime fair Hope-maiden, who roamed free
Among the flowers, till Hell's arch-lord, Default,
Swept me down, down, to the dark ante-vault
Where, after long droughts, parchings past belief,
They offered me the pomegranate . . . I knew
The hard condition, yet I cried, I too,
    "Only relief". . . Ah (you
Who know) feel, feel now what this one relief
Will mean, whose taking shall destroy your place
In the bright world, shall prison you in gloom,
Shall wed you to remorse . . . Look on my face,
Friend, I implore you . . . Guess that lord, that home . . .'

26
Drought

The shadeless elms, the poplars shimmerless
Have yellowed, dropped their flaccid leaves a full
Two months before their time; the alder-pool
Is a black miry swamp, ploughed by the press
Of tortured, thirsty cattle; or look where
Once would a spreading line of verdure show
The river's lush umbrageous path, that now
Is a hard white road, hedged with willows bare.

Autumn will flush no harvest in these fields
Failed of slow Nature's sober, ripening clime,
Nor winter in these woods brighten with rime
Red berry, brown nut, her late-lavished yields

To bird and beast: the blighted copse they rob
Already of its last lean hip and cob.

On the wings unseen
   Of chance's breaths
Borne are we between
   Life's world and death's;

On the trembling cord
   Of our frail will
Walk 'neath God's high word
   O'er deepest ill;

And through all that parts
   Glad heaven from hell
Quicklier fall our hearts
   Than tongue can tell.

Children of wealth in your warm nursery,
Set in the cushioned window-seat to watch
The volleying snow, guarded invisibly
By the clear double pane through which no touch
Untimely penetrates, you cannot tell
What winter means; its cruel truths to you
Are only sound and sight; your citadel
Is safe from feeling, and from knowledge too.

Go down, go out to elemental wrong,
Waste your too round limbs, tan your skin too white;
The glass of comfort, ignorance, seems strong
Today, and yet perhaps this very night

You'll wake to horror's wrecking fire — your home
Is wired within for this, in every room.

The servant-girl sleeps. By the small low bed,
On the mean chest of drawers, are carefully
Arranged her poor belongings — photos spread
Cross-wise, a box of tawdry jewelry . . .
Outside the airless attic looms the vast
Of sultry night; huge clouds are mounting, fraught
With lurid flashes . . . Look! A tremor passed
Over the tired face, as of anxious thought.

Is it of lightning tragedy she dreams?
Is it of darkly louring pain and care?
What profound unrest to her pent soul seems
To gloom the world? *'On Sunday shall I wear*

The white? . . . It's less becoming . . . but the blue
Is last year's fashion now . . . and faded, too.'

30
Still-Life

Through the open French window the warm sun
lights up the polished breakfast-table, laid
round a bowl of crimson roses, for one —
a service of Worcester porcelain, arrayed
near it a melon, peaches, figs, small hot
rolls in a napkin, fairy rack of toast,
butter in ice, high silver coffee pot,
and, heaped on a salver, the morning's post.

She comes over the lawn, the young heiress,
from her early walk in her garden-wood
feeling that life's a table set to bless
her delicate desires with all that's good,

that even the unopened future lies
like a love-letter, full of sweet surprise.

All that shall ne'er be thine,
　　Beauty, maybe, or love,
Wealth, or the power whose wine
　　Lifts thee the world above,

Branches whose nectar-fruit
　　Thou canst but smell and see,
The flowery Eden-plot
　　By fate forbidden thee —

Wan loiterer, beware:
　　Thy road unnatural
Is haunted — whispers there
　　The subtlest snake of all —

Thou, with God's chosen few,
　　Abjurest poisoned lust:
Thou scorn'st as angels do
　　The garland that's but dust.

32
Frustration

God granted, God denies —
    So faith has said;
But fonder faith still cries
    Uncomforted.

Now are thy labours o'er —
    But hope says: 'These
That make me, love I more
    Than barren ease.'

Still shalt thou glorify
    Thy God — Nay, still
Bends desire but to *my*
    Creating will.

33
Blind

Patience, the woman that attends on me,
That every morning sweeps my soul's dark room,
Ranges the thought that hangs where light should be,
Prepares for sense its sustenance of gloom —
Patience, the care-taker drear-voiced and sour,
Of ways abstemious, of small wishes few,
The plodding creature that must every hour
Return and rectify whate'er I do —

Patience, that has but one consoling word,
One same grey comfort for my sorrow black,
Mutt'ring the hard text that so oft I've heard:
All highest wealth is won from lowest lack —

She wearies me to death, and yet I know
That for my life I dare not bid her go.

You who are blest, say this: 'The canvas blank
That's my free life, the years without one line
Drawn on them of restraint, for which I thank
My God, he gave me that I should design
Bold vivid beauty — should my soul imbrue
In its own blood, kill self — or feel the sword
Of cruellest failure's conquering.' . . . But you,
Curst in pain's prison, say: 'I praise my Lord
That he the sombre plan did not refuse
To limn — has left me but the simpler work
Of filling up the outline, with what hues
I may of sober patience, colours dark

Of courage — that he keeps me from the stress,
The anguished dangers, of unhinderedness.'

Ambition

Another day held out by future's hand,
Another strung on past's assembling thread,
To its eternal place in order led,
A graded pearl upon a necklace planned;
Small were the orbs at first, of value small,
Then slowly waxed, became the precious row
Which, waxing still, must yet ere long, I know
Wane to their worthlessness original.

Another day's work set on the fine cord
Of willed intent, that shall or beauty bring
To clasped completion, or, too frail, shall fling
Away of all my pains the one reward —

The gift that with time's gifts I would create,
To which all thoughts, words, deeds I dedicate.

God's light is, to guess
   (where you have not been)
brighter fieriness,

passionately to fight
   till the splendour seen
is your place by right,

to pass on, look back
   at glory . . . discern
only deepest black . . .

Need, fatigue, shame — three
   Hells wherein to burn . . .
   This is toil's return,
   this the heaven we earn
everlastingly.

What is a summer day? A century —
More than a life-span — all of golden prime,
Of power, of brilliance, urging, burning me
To save, translate it as immortal rhyme;
It is a continent, from pole to pole
(From mist-white dawn to evening) all the way
A paradise, wherein the scenes unroll
Of warmth, of wonderment too sweet to say.

It is what leads to hours more amorous still,
To dusk's even lovelier gardens, where again,
Like wafts essential that the soul o'er-fill,
Passions seem almost poesy . . . ah then

To the dark paths like naught but death — despair
At light, life, love that I cannot declare.

38
The Enchantress

The moon lay on her couch of cloud
   Above the gloomed floor of the land,
Under the darkening arch where glowed
   Now distantly the glory banned . . .

Veiled was the dais of the downs
   Lost was the well-known line between
The embers of the living towns,
   The star-lamps of where heaven had been,

And she that is nor present love
   Nor memoried, neither flesh nor soul,
Smiled . . . smiled . . . *'The future will I move,*
   Creation's seas will I control.'

    Have you noticed
The slim buds of the beech, how first they bend
Sun-wards, then, almost visibly, extend
    To be warm-kissed
Their finger-fans . . . how soon attain their tender prime
The lucent leaf-throngs that aloft in softness blend? . . .
'Ah, yes, I have a pass to fancy's amorous clime.'

    Or has bracken
Shown you, first, proud heads bowed, then a scant band
Of forms strained but ecstatic . . . then, full-manned
    Fern-armies, green
Gold, gory? . . . 'Shall no faery strifes attend my state
To whom belongs now every season's passionate land? —
Who therefore stiffly walk, salute nor love nor hate.'

O tragic world of dark and stars,
  Of splendours wasted on the void,
Of weary, ever-circling wars,
  Of hopes new-lit and hopes destroyed,

O glorious world of sun and flowers,
  Of passions freed in perfect form,
Of ever-fresh triumphant powers,
  Of living grace, of grandeur warm —

My soul has thrown his window wide,
  And soared into your boundless grief;
My heart has to her garden hied
  And roamed your rapture past belief,

Who now returned to their small room
  Sit talking in the twilight grey —
Wonder: 'Which was the dream? . . . the gloom,
  Then, or the gladness? . . . night or day?'

I know
That death's in ambush everywhere I go,
With bow full-bent
To strike my sluggard powers ere they be spent:

I know
That waits he for my loved ones even so,
And, when he'll smite,
Shall stab me too, shall faulty love requite;

Yet still
To mind's affirming, deaf is slothful will:
Still lax and vain
Is heart, nor hears how memory weeps amain.

Fresh spring, in whose deep woods I sought,
    As in your cool abodes I played,
The phantoms of my childish thought,
    The spirits of the faery shade;

Warm summer, in whose fields I met
    My fancy's every fond device,
Where small imagination set
    The very scenes of Paradise;

Now are your forests high the hall
    Of shades more surely fugitive;
Now raptures lost beyond recall
    In your unsunned recesses live;

Now to your cloudless meadows come
    Forms lit with longing's fiercest flame;
Now truly are your haunts their home
    Eternal, whom with tears I name.

43
Bye-Flowers

You who to the copse are gone,
   You who haunt the orchard-rill,
Whose shy graces are outshone
   By the bolder daffodil;

You who near the river's edge
   Stand like modest maidens tall,
Crowded by the ousting sedge,
   Slim waifs of the waterfall;

You who the hard stubble-field
   Have with flaunting poppy shared,
You who make the hedge a shield,
   Blindly by the mower spared;

You who live with the lean grass
   Of the wind-worn, chalky down,
So diminished that men pass
   Your sweet faces by unknown —

Ah, not lightly may I speak
   Your too well remembered names,
Your once starry beauties seek
   That now like loved living flames

Prick each scene familiar, glow
   Warm as his far look intent,
Who my childhood taught to know
   Your fair hidden firmament.

I led into the silent room
    The stranger, waited there
Beside him who for this had come
    From his far hemisphere.

The ordered books, the desk full-strewn,
    The faded curtain green
Tempering the sun of afternoon,
    All was as it had been

But that the air, inhumed and hushed,
    Was of no earthly clime —
I stood, but my claimed spirit rushed
    Back, back o'er seas of time.

I heard the pilgrim's movéd speech,
    My measured speech, as hears
One havened in the past the beach
    Where break rough present's years.

Farewell for a while,
    My lov'd one, only;
For earth's little mile
    Of pathway lonely;

For one weary march
    Of sense's pining,
Driv'n out from the arch
    Of joy's enshrining;

For one journey short
    Of thought's sore bearing,
Expelled from the fort
    Of sorrow's sharing;

Till once more the height
    Of truth attainéd,
I'll see the lost light
    Of love unwanéd,

Where (so longing saith)
    Life's road shall leave me —
No more, mortal death,
    Shalt thou deceive me.

(For M. M. B., April 1932.)

As, those hours of sorrow ended,
  Gave we up — 'twas his desire —
Our loved burden, nor defended
  Our faint spirits from the fire,
    But in fierce destruction sharing,
    Purged our mortal need's despairing,

So, to our changed home returning,
  Left we what he bade us leave;
With hearts full, yet not of yearning,
  Too exalted now to grieve,
    Giving thanks, our tears then stayed we —
    So, too, his behest obeyed we.

Harebell of the idle hill,
 Cockle of industrious corn,
Meadowsweet of laughing rill,
 Restharrow of heath forlorn,
  Are for her whose quiet face
  Welcome is in every place.

Poppy crimson, scarlet too,
 Marigold whose bluish green
Leads to cornflower's primal blue,
 Scabious, mallow, here shall mean
  Her whose simple spirit white
  Is the sum of all that's bright.

So at end of summer we,
 Gathering symbols for her, say
What with the soul's eye we see;
 So too, now, this prayer will pray —
  That she whom love warmed shall bless,
  Blooming long, our sunlessness.

(For M. M. B., August 31, 1931.)

You should at times go out
    from where the faithful kneel,
visit the slums of doubt
    and feel what the lost feel;

you should at times walk on,
    away from your friends' ways,
go where the scorned have gone,
    pass beyond blame and praise;

and at times you should quit
    (ah yes) your sunny home,
sadly awhile should sit,
    even, in wrong's dark room,

or ever, suddenly
    by simple bliss betrayed,
you shall be forced to flee,
    unloved, alone, afraid.

49
For —

If your loved one prove unworthy, why then,
by this much you're the freer: if the block
to which you're bolted warp and shrink away,
why then, it only gives you further play,
makes life rough for you, of course, with its knock
and rattle, with defection's loud sudden
jars, but your own quiet integrity,
tried thus the more, has but more room to be.

So says one truth, but soon says another:
Now in your soul-tissues a wrong sap stains
the white rose that you were; your heart sustains
the wild-thorn traits of your grafted partner:
when the mistaken marriage mortifies,
it's your own branch and stem and root that dies.

Today was the drear song of Nature's mood
     My monody;
The mournful soul of wind and rain and wood
     Was one with me:

Under the straining trees whose tortured power
     Was my pride's own,
I walked the wildered wood-paths, hour on hour,
     By anger blown,

Until with night-calm came fatigue's calm too
     Darkly to bless
Will's stubborn forms; thought's worn ways, fading, knew
     Forgetfulness.

Throstle in the wood,
    you know everything
or hurtful or good
    that a lad's feeling;

you know what I feel
    when I bend to take
a sweet cowslip, kneel
    the first, for its sake;

you know what it means
    to find an orchid,
you know what happens
    when whitethorn's sighted;

you know what I know,
    too, of the dark thorn,
you knew long ago
    before I was born —

throstle in the wood,
    you know everything
or painful or good
    of a lover's spring.

52
Forbidden Love
(For Constance)

If you were not what I know you to be,
(my knight) whose tower of control baffles me,
outside whose bolted and defended gates,
wide-eyed but dumb, my wistful spirit waits,
as a mourner waits by a rock-sealed tomb
for one who comes not, nor can ever come;

if you did not as you do — if you came,
sallied out only a little, to claim
what you know is yours — then it would be I,
(as *I* know that *you* know) who'd fortify
perforce my dwelling, dart sternness at you,
fight you as now I have no need to do.

Were *your* love other than it is, and *my*
love other, they would either force or fly
the deadlock, and, so doing, each would kill
the other, that now from firm walls of will
look friendly, calmly, unafraid to face
even each other, from that high, safe place.

Is this then grandeur, says the sun —
To look down on the dwindled world
Whose tiny high and low are one?

Is this then radiance — to be furled
In small earth-urging rounds, to bend
My beams to things that I transcend?

Is this sublimity — to rule
Among soulless inferiors,
Myself but of myself the tool,

Unsummoned by diviner spheres —
To fire *me*, draw *me* there is none —
Is this all heaven then, says the sun?

Anger, last enemy,
That the long fight has but increased, not killed,
    Fiend racking, piercing me
With thoughts of life's morn-promise unfulfilled,

    Night-mood that first I knew
As a mere dusk that dulled my sunny dreams,
    Then, ever deepening, grew
To glooms unfathomed, stabbed with passionate gleams,

    Ah, how can a soul slay
(Nor slay, too, love itself) your lust love-driven?
    How end your hell, nor say:
'You too are naught, all zeal's high starry heaven'?

How long, said spirit, must I walk this earth?
I, wingéd, to whom Paradise gave birth,
how long must I pace fields of drought and dearth?

How long, said mind, must I tread the small maze
of paths bewild'ring, of thought that betrays
my straight endeavour with blind-alleyed ways?

How long must I, said life, said bodied soul,
be baulked by faulty flesh from beauty's goal?
How long have but pittance, who see joy's whole?

How long, said heart, may I love's raiment wear?
How long may I work for those I hold dear?
When must I leave them in sorrow and fear?

I sought, sought for my sweet —
   She cannot be here,
I found but her void seat
   And her empty lair;

I called, called for my love —
   She must be away,
Silent is her cool grove
   And her garden gay.

With straining eyes I've sought,
   I've heark'd with strain'd ears,
As one with doubts distraught,
   One fevered with fears,

As one who shudd'ring drinks
   But half bitter truth,
As one who sips, then shrinks
   From sharp, scalding ruth,

As one who sorrow sees
   But in fancy hides,
Who the wrecked present flees,
   In the past abides.

Suspense has drained all savour from these hours . . .
The fierce sun, poised above our fevered clime
(Moving but imperceptibly as time
Forces it on) still from its filled sky glowers
Insatiate, parches fragrant blooms to dust,
Sucks the sap even from thorns, thirstily kills
All flesh but serpents' — our soft life distils
Of formed desires into one boundless lust.

Travellers of earth's worst desert we toil on,
Worn tough, narrowed by torments to endure
All that once seemed too much for us, and more.
Pleasure, love, beauty are a palmy town

Beyond our grim horizon . . . we forget
Their sunset-land . . . our anguish will not set.

O strong to bless
human misery,
sweet lovingkindness
comfort thou me:

thou who alone
mortal hurt canst heal,
most merciful one
to thee I kneel.

Though man may set
his soul to harsh ill,
despising thee, yet
thou lovest still:

yea, though he spurn
thee, leave thee, yet thou
patient, his return
awaitest — now

to us, heart-sore,
solace give; now we,
Mother, yet once more
come home to thee.

The Prodigal

I will arise, for I have climbed too far,
I will abase me, whose descent is done;
I will be fearless, who have failed in war,
I will surrender, who my fight have won;
I will be born, for of youth's petty breath
I now am weary, and of puny pride;
I will be slain, for with desire's long death
I am despaired, and would with love abide.

I will arise and, to my place returned,
Will stand up to my guilt, will, bold no less,
Bow down to what, before, my folly spurned,
Will humble me to nature, will confess

That I have risen against heaven; I have wronged
The lowly home where I of right belonged.

The heavens are lost in fog; a fog-wall hides
All but the nearest bushes, and divides
Dank lawn from sodden meadow, from drear plains
Where now, I know, only crushed grass remains
And broken thistles, and, on thorn-brakes bare,
Wreckage of rotted briony; I stare
From the blank window; steady-dripping eves
Mark off the moments; soul its doom perceives.

It was not yesterday, that day we stood
('Twas endless years ago) in a warm wood
One with the snowdrop army — shimmery spears
And shining helmets, pure young pioneers
Climbing the slope — Ah, yes, that was the day
Of dauntless white, not of defeated grey.

Alone with staring thought
   I watched the white clouds fly,
I saw what morn had brought
   Pass from the darkening sky.

Alone with my last friend
   I watched the visions fade,
I saw life's sun descend
   Into a soul-less shade.

Sunless November, how hast thou now turned
To drear appraisement all our glad employ!
Chill visitor, who com'st but to destroy
With one sad look our summer-wealth late earned
Of glorious bloom; silent remembrancer,
Who, hand on lip, with haunting eye dost tell
To hill and field and wood what know they well —
How changéd shall they be from what they were.

Now, taught beyond her leafy joys, each tree
Lets fall those first that were the first to grow,
Dulling thy steps, as by each dank hedgerow
Of perished grace thou walk'st: now echoes thee
Down the dim alleys of each mind the slow
The muffled footfall of eternity.

I saw heaven opened — ah, it was not Heaven,
    That cold, pale place whence very silence cried:
'Woe to the world that for a god has striven,
    Woe to the hosts that for a dream have died,
            Woe . . . Woe . . .
To ardour that has wrought but its own overthrow. . .'

I saw the doors of heaven wrenched off — no glare
    Of glory assailed me; from that lidless eye
Unmoving came only the chill dull stare
    Of strangely fissured clouds, of leaky sky
            That kept my sight
Searching, yet blessed it never with coherent light.

Then breathed the voice that was no voice — all round
    From weird-lit stillness (as before the screams,
Crashes, dust-hazes of an earthquake, sound
    Is hushed, stars shine clearer) from those dumb gleams
            Exhaled a cry;
Thought's coming thunder flashed a vivid prophecy —

'Woe to the body dogged with useless sense,
    Woe to the heart martyred for beauty vain,
Woe to the mind fighting for truth's pretence,
    Woe to the soul — ah, yes, even fierier pain,
            Even deeper woe
To the doomed soul . . . fierce, endless shall be her
                                            death-throe;

'For as the hero in his final hour
    Embraces an eternity of bliss,

One with bright faith, possessed by blinding power,
    Sees not annihilation's near abyss,
        So slain belief
Tastes at the last an immortality of grief;

    'And still, to mock man's agony, the sun
      Shall shine through mindless leaves, unfeeling birds
Shall sing, and as on this May morn his own
      Warm blood's sabbath-bells shall peal, peal with words
        Of happiness
That is not save for such low things — is reasonless.'

Any storm is peace
   if it stops a fight;
to end war-service
   a wound is delight . . .

To greatest grief, then,
   come, all lesser grief —
to heaven hell-shaken
   earth-shocks are relief;

any wild life-sea
   stills the soul astrain,
all pangs of body
   ease a mind in pain.

65

Now that delight is seen for what she is,
    A half-wit dancing while her home's afire,
Now that of doting hope the melodies
    Are drowned in thunders, that simple desire
        Who spread her feast
On a volcano has decamped, scared like a beast,

Yes, now that every tenderness is naught
    Whereby hard Nature won us to her will
Who has at last o'erreached herself, has wrought
    The self-destroying bomb of human skill
        Unhallowed, how
Shall man's lorn soul be aided? Who shall save him now?

One only is there, though defiance too
    Is mortal, though even stubborn pride must die,
One that with engined wings lifts to the blue
    Of a bare heaven, whence, under its smoke-sky,
        Earth pales, is made
Merely a phantom background for his own firm shade.

No wall of fate, no pain's imprisoning bar
Shall break the patience of my stronger will;
No water quench its fire, no fire the far-
Flung warring of its ordered tides distil;
Nor any forceful storm do aught but fan
Its tempering breaths that through my being blow . . .
But how I so can hold me, how thus can
Be my own keeper, is not mine to know.

Not all creation's powers can now remove —
Not death itself — the stateless flag that flies
Mast-nailed, the hard-lashed helm that I approve . . .
But ask me why, for what strange paradise
I've set me so, this only can I tell:
That to swerve but one hair's breadth, this is Hell.

From some dead moon a feeble ray
   Came through my thinly parted cloud,
And said: 'Thou'lt see no more the day,
   O yearner wild, O captive proud,

But with this glimmer I'll re-start
   From torpor's pallet thy despair;
I'll set once more thy starving heart
   A-search around her chamber bare.'

Christmas eve — a scene
of hoar-gleams and snow . . .
What does whiteness mean?
What does winter show?

Come into the woods,
see the wonder-change;
on everything broods
   a beauty strange;

every twig is soft
   and furred with light,
every bud a tuft
   of feathers bright,

every branch is thick
   and crystal-mossed —
this is the magic
   of fog and frost;

when the heavens are dank,
   the lands icy,
earth is on the brink
of a mystery . . .

Glory will not last,
peace is only snow,
look at the dark past,
force feeling to know;

faith's a dripping tree,
wonder melts away,
this is what you see,
what you dare not say . . .

For us who are tired
with truth-light, with cold
now the day, pale-fired,
   ends as of old;

like numbed things that creep
   under dead leaves,
    let us sleep, sleep,
lost to all that grieves,

hid from hard winter's
sun white as a moon,
far from midnight fears
and madness of noon,

safe from beauty's scene,
its hoar-gleams and snow —
from all that has been,
is, shall be, of woe.

Forbidding land
Where finds my flesh no food,
   Whose salty strand
Is bare of body's good,

   On whose waste plain
My hungry heart has pined,
   Who feed'st in vain
With thorns my weary mind,

   Through thee's the track
To heights of heavenly rest —
   Most fearéd Lack
Thou from beyond art blest.

Life's a bird can breathe the air
Of misery's upland bare,
Even of icy-peaked despair;

Life's a bird can build her nest
On the rock-ledge of unrest,
Close to cliffy danger's crest;

A strong bird whose patient brood
Thrive on scant, on bloody food
From disaster's solitude.

Of whom if not of these, then, should I sing?
To whom but these hold up the altering glass
Wherein (for so we nature can surpass)
I may create their happier imaging?
To whom, if not to those unlovely ones,
Will's lawless host, dark angels who through pride,
Through aspiration too instant to hide,
Are fall'n for ever, damned with him who shuns
Obedient Heav'n, as him by self's disease
Blemished, deformed, powerless now but to turn
Others likewise to what for aye must burn
In its own Hell . . . To whom if not to these?

For temperance — all that's devoutly strong —
Needs no art, is its own celestial song.

From day to converse night, from night to day,
Often I've turned, not as from dark to light,
But as from glory of day to peace of night,
From drear of night to noon's tormenting ray;
Till know I not from which I now should pray
For rescue, strenuous plight or stagnant plight,
Nor whether angry right or easy right
Be better, how to balance way with way.

Helper there's none on the all-risking road,
For heaven's own gambler there's nor guard nor guide:
No rest is there, save for him who can hide
In his own grey dispassion's tent-abode;
No rapture but for him who wills to ride
The fiery steed that's but on zeal bestowed.

There is o'ermuch that eagerness would do;
Small time, low strength, that home the labourer
Have trammelled him for life; he cannot stir
From his allotment, from his chattels few;
Yet endless skies are over him; day-through
Their visions to his craving eyes recur;
Each morn his looks of longing will confer
With vast imagination's orient view.

How may he feel full passion's tropic sun?
How live with arctic wisdom's nightless blaze,
Nor leave the while, under pale duty's rays,
Her temperate paths? O, how, too, follow one,
Most wise, most fiery Poesy, whose ways
Are dark to him who has all these not done?

Song

To one I turn my face,
   For 'tis her lawful due;
The other I embrace,
   And what she bids I do.

To one I give my hand,
   To one I give my heart;
By one I'm bound to stand,
   From one I'll never part.

One keeps my mortal home,
   My safety's anxious wife;
With my mistress I roam
   Nor reck of death nor life.

One's calléd earthly care,
   The other, heavenly bliss;
And who is he can share
   With both, perfection's kiss?

New Year's Eve

Launch we the ship of the new year, launch her by night,
By light of the high young moon and the stars' far light
That's white and tremulous; turn her bows to the east
Where soon is to break the dawn of her birthday feast —
Soon, O her venturing hopes, shall receive you the wide
Ocean, the sun-lit future, its shadowless tide.

Bring in the ship of the old year, bring her by dark,
By dim of the waning moon and the sinking spark
Of war's fiery planet; heave her in with her crew
Of weary desires, of wishes that won not through —
Let her lie with her sister-ships; now opens slowly the vast
Harbour its gates for her; takes her the sombre past.

Once more, brave morning, bring'st thou here
The shining shield, the new-whet spear:
Once more I take refreshed from thee
My life's familiar armoury.

Once more with bright eyes I behold
The bloomy mist on mountains old,
With eagerness restored I gaze
Where duly thou'lt the curtain raise

On fate's laid scene: nor the cord slips
From thy sure grasp, nor move thy lips,
But in thine endless look is all
That has befall'n, that shall befall.

Fear not lest the morrow bring
On her wild-imagined wing
Storms to spoil thy harvesting:

Fear not lest she fail to throw
Beams propitious, who the bow
Did of lofty promise show:

Fear not, though thou never wield
Fame's low sickle: fair's thy yield,
Thou that till'st in faith thy field.

The lily said: I labour not to know
What wonders may be in the world beyond;
I look but where my lord has planted me . . .

I care not from what sources strange may flow
The streams that feed me, what mysterious bond
Has solemn rain, or soft dew-alchemy;

Nor in what glooms are quickening airs begun,
What charter has the spring breeze, or the strong
Warm summer-breath that now about me stirs;

Enough that on my beauty beauty's sun
Looks every day more ardently, more long,
Saying: 'What sweetness is arrayed like hers?'

Low spoke she, meekly bending. In the press
Half hid she was, of lilies numberless.

I will hold out my arms
   To spring who clothes me
     (Says the beech),
To kind summer who warms
   My room and soothes me;
     I will reach
For rich autumn's robe, red
   With pride and grieving;
     I will hold
Out my worn dress for dread
   Winter's unweaving
     In the cold.

Ten years, perhaps, or twenty — at the most
Less than two score — shall surely terminate
Your lease of Eden, and unloving fate
Shall launch you forth from the enchanted coast . . .
Is this your lot? One brief hour more of ease,
A garden-walk foreshortened now by fear,
Its forms and odours torturingly dear
To you whose long home is the lifeless seas,

Or this? — An age of struggle on the slope
Of failure's pit, that's deep as the sublime
Clift's high of what you've set yourself, a time
When naught is real save rock and axe and rope,

And the kind angel-voice that cries at last:
'Rest, for the perils of ascent are passed.'

Well, and what of it? What if you are beautiful?
What if your ready mirror show you hour by hour
far eyes profound as a heaven-reflecting pool,
mouth like the rainbow's smile upon the summer shower?
What if your faithful thirsty lovers think of you
as of some draught celestial, some pure passion's wine,
when still the man-made Grail of their adoring view
flows but with vanity, ferment of worldly vine?

Is this achievement? Is this what shall make you glad?
Is this a gift for others bought with your life-blood,
a sweet truth that shall warm men's starving hearts,
                                       shall add
to weal, this cold, corroding misuse of rich good?

Out on you, woman: quit your beauty, ere the day
when what's within it shall have eat'n it all away.

82
For —

It is pleasant to hang out
this sign at your open gate:
'Succour for the desolate' —
your neighbours praise you, no doubt;

but woe to whoe'er in need
at the inner door has knocked,
found the snug room barred and locked
where alone you fatly feed.

The woman I'd revere
would be a warm hearth-fire,
not a chilly taper
posed for all to admire,
   a white saint in the gloom,
   but the heart of a home,

a soul burning to bless
its circle, spent for cheer,
a life-giver, thoughtless
how its own life appear,
   whether itself may seem
   a fair or formless gleam.

And the man I'd love, too,
though he'd be a sure light
in the house, a help through
the things of trouble's night,
   would be more than a tame
   measured glow without flame,

one who'd be now and then
o'ercharged with primal power,
a sudden, a rushing
flash in oppression's hour,
   wrath's lightning, rightly hurled,
   the dread of wrong's dark world.

A squalid July street, a sweaty crowd,
Shop-staring, jostling . . . That was the mean frame,
The picture, this — a girl whose bearing showed,
Like a cool background, all from whence she came,
Her spacious, quiet home . . . A coarse, wide hat,
Black-ribboned, cast in shade the exquisite
Pale profile, frail beside the massive plait,
Waist-long, of flaxen glory gathered tight.

I thought: 'Such beauty were a magic boat
Whereby a woman's heart might make its truce
With fate, idly, in its own bliss afloat' —
Forgot how even as honour has no use

For honours, beauty, too, that's of the mind
Sees only tasks, is to its mirror blind.

Eyes that queenly sit
   At their casement wide,
Mouth that holdeth it
   As a sentry tried,

For the rest, the face
   Howso built it be,
'Tis the fair palace
   Of fair majesty.

Be the friendly house
   Castle high or cot,
Mean or sumptuous,
   Spirit careth not,

If but strength shall show
   At the guarded gate;
If but the window
   Love illuminate.

When your work's done, banish it behind you,
forget its beauties and its failures both;
you've done your part by the child, borne, bred it,
given it your blood, at your heart fed it,
clothed it with care, taught it your hard-learned truth;
now that it's grown let nothing remind you
of what's for ever made lovely, or marred —
no, turn to what's still in your power to guard.

Visit not often the past that bore you,
nor the too-friendly pleasures at your gate,
nor your soul's offspring wedded to their fate —
keep your house, the every need procure you

of those to come, your works yet to be born;
toil, plan and pray for them noon, night and morn.

What though many praise me
    for my imperfect song?
They'll only deafen me
    to the notes that are wrong.

What though a few, fondly,
    weave me a garland rare?
I'll sing but drowsily
    in the scent-laden air.

What though my heart even
    whisper at length: 'Well done!' —
God grant I'll drink not then
    thy wine, fell poisoning one!

St. Nicholas
(Isle of Thanet)

The wide road from the city runs
    A furlong from her doors,
And every hurrying tradesman shuns
    Her track unkempt, ignores

The old bleak hamlet, that apart
    Lives her enduring days,
Whose blunt flint tower, uncouth and swart,
    Nor storm nor time decays.

Above her nettly gardens still
    Her knotted elms oppose
Gales whose ungovernable will
    The trim town never knows,

And past her meagre fields the blanked
    The viewless distance tells
Where, fronting ocean's roar, are ranked
    Her cliffs' dumb sentinels.

Tell not thy trouble to that child, the morn,
For she'll to folly win thee unawares;
Nor to noon's amazon who hotly dares,
And thy cool sanity will swift suborn;
Nor to the nun whose ardours quenched are sworn
To twilight peace, nor to her who impairs
More than they all, with her black, blank despairs,
Celestial truth, and leaves thy world forlorn.

Nay; to no mortal hour of gloom or glee
Incline thee; yet awhile let each one look
On what's to hand; their admonitions brook,
Give ear awhile to every plaint and plea:
Forget then feeling's counsellors; turn thee
To thine own place; write all in wisdom's book.

Winter Larches

Beyond the firs thick-curtained from the blast,
that hoard in their close unlit house a few
half-rotted cones, brown rags of bracken — past
the draughty ruins of the oaks, that strew
their dank drear courts with wreckage, past the cold
unroofed aisles of the beeches, see how here
the larches standing on their sober gold —
the slow-shed beauty that they wrought and share —
live without shadows in the sunny place
that's of their own making, and a moonlight
of silver lichen on each column's face
shows where it met, scarce moving and upright,

the worst winds . . . Yes, strange timeless beams illume
these halls; here we forget November gloom.

We have seen endangered ships
 Driven by the hounding blast,
Rushing from the tooth that strips
 Canvas racked from lurching mast . . .
 On the cradling waves we rest:
 Borne are we on safety's breast.

We have watched their progress slow
 When the deadly calm prevailed,
When they grappled with the foe
 Step by short step, heavy-sailed . . .
 We have watched from where we ride
 Curvetting, on aery tide.

Here, where the larks sing, and the sun's so warm
That gorse-pods click each minute, and the grass
Rustles, as through dry bents the breezes pass,
And butterflies over the heather swarm,
Here I, an ardent lover of all these,
Would build our home — I'd take but the small crest
Of the long hill, and leave untouched the rest,
The coney-shaven turf, the scanty trees.

Here, having marked and worked our cottage-claim,
We'd meet the first shy rays, on summer dawns,
Approaching to unveil our dewy lawns
Of wild-flowers; and when winter evenings came,

We'd watch from our bright room the stealthy dark
Muffling the stunt thorns of our snowy park.

Wherefore solicit
   for your daily bread?
The day will bring it,
   will the table spread

that gives ere you ask
   all you need, no less,
to perform your task
   of hard forgiveness.

A morsel of good,
   a dole too of wrong,
is the simple food
   that makes mercy strong;

of joy a small sip,
   of trouble a share,
is all that friendship
   takes to make her fair.

Wild thoughts that once would fly like homing birds
To a far place, I've caught and tamed you now,
Nor struggle ye more 'gainst my caging words,
But ever meeker, more accustomed grow;
Now are ye hooded hawks whose eager eyes
See only their hard lord's intended prey,
Nor ever for themselves hunt out a prize,
Nor back to their own native region stray.

Here, as there, with a swing of golden doors,
Dawn shall invite to day's long dusty road;
Here, full as comfortingly, dusk restores
Tired flesh in her all-welcoming abode;

Here, too, may needy spirit find again
Cheer's morn, mercy's night, in the hearts of men.

Once more, light-bringer,
    with unfailing brand,
wake your worshipper
    to understand;

though in the shadow
    winter's haunting near,
on the bright meadow
    falls not a fear;

in the warm wood now
    between grief and grief
blithe is every bough
    and every leaf;

though death's behind me,
    death not far before,
undying beauty
    is at my door.

Plant no poppy (he said)
no frail lily sublime,
for in war's famine-time
thou'lt need but corn for bread.

Hoard no jewel (he cried)
no dazzling laboured gem:
thou'lt be forced to sell them
for steel, so now decide.

Set no flower in thy word
(he besought, but none heard)
cut no flash to thy wit,
if thou must disown it
when seest thou sorrow's sword.

For my misdeed I blame my erring friend's
No faultier imperfection; so too he
Thrusts back the taunt on one who in turn sends
It farther still; then fancy, winging free,
Bears it on, till, beyond earth's blackened past,
On blameless power primordial lies the blame,
Till on eternal shores my times are cast,
And glory immortal heaped with mortal shame.

Then says the angel, says the ardent soul
That stands above me: 'Is not this then proof,
Impious blasphemer, that the wrong's control
Rests but with thee, — that 'neath thine own low roof

Is born, abides, thy sin? Call then a halt
To visiting of blame: take home thy fault.'

This is the sword
That you shall wield for me (says the world-lord)

Not that soiled arm,
The scimitar of vengeance, bent for harm,

Not what relies
On a cross-hilt held up to exorcize,

No, the soul-pain
That you shall wield has clean sharp edges twain . . .

Wound, grieve all men,
Scourge the unworthy in earth's temple, then

Say (grieving too)
'Forgive them, for they know not what they do'.

September

Now the sun's more tender gaze
    Lingers on the land he leaves,
Gilds with ghostly harvest-haze
    Stubble wan and drooping sheaves;

Now in every hedgerow twine,
    Fiery as a farewell bliss,
Flame-leafed briony, the vine,
    Turned to smoke, of clematis;

Now beside the silent stream
    Loosestrife lights her candle tall;
Now the yellowing aspens seem
    High pyres of a funeral

Where from her low couch the mist
    Rises, sighing like a wraith:
'With thy grieving hast thou kissed
    Thy dear follower to death.'

Faithless familiars,
    summer friends untrue,
once-dear beguilers,
    now wave ye adieu:

swift warmth and beauty
    who awhile had won
my glad company
    I watch you pass on.

Now the still hearth-fire
    intently gloweth,
now weary desire
    her dwelling knoweth,

now a newly-lit
    lamp afar shall burn,
the roving spirit
    stay her, and return.

Long, than a hair more slender, is the bridge
Set for thy saving: from the first high land
Whence saw'st thou good and evil is it spanned —
The crest of contemplation's lonely ridge;
There, whence a myriad tortuous paths go down,
It soars in one bold arch above the earth,
Sweeps o'er the dwindled plains of wealth and dearth,
The oceans of disaster. and renown.

Gloomed is the road between the soul and God,
Set beyond vision's reach or thought's assay,
Yet failed it never him who all the way
Held the rope-rail of patience, and had shod

His feet with sureness, nor the lamp did scorn
That his forefathers lit ere he was born.

October

Now the misty elm-trees stand
Row on row across the vale,
Wardens of a windless land,

By deserted fields, that, pale,
Tell of labour's met demand,
Of heaped ricks and home-travail

Where the steady engine hums:
Now to the still valley comes
Calm of harvest, peace that's knit

Of long weariness, and throws
Softness o'er the tired spirit,
Veils with sleep her worn meadows —

O breeze of our bare hillside,
Sound no more in urgence those
Fresh tales of a world more wide!

103
The Waterfall
(For R. C.)

We traced our river up the rich defiles
That home its tropic flow a hundred miles
From human habitation . . . Bend on bend,
Each brought the same image — a mirror-end
Curtained by verdure . . . not a hut, a boat,
Broke the lone scene, the silence not a shout,
Plash-song of paddle, grunt of rowlocked oar . . .
Only the tiny flying fish would score
The surface with their flashes, quick as dreams,
Or, rending some deep thicket, shrill as sudden doubt,
The harsh macaws would start us with their haunting
screams.

Day after day the muffled pulsings rose
From the hot engine — steadily their dirge
Told our slow passage — till at last the gorge
Steepened, grew barer, seemed about to close,
To block our way . . . we sensed an end, a wall . . .
Then a roar said: 'Behold your goal, the Waterfall' . . .

A thousand feet of torn stream falling sheer
In fog and thunder . . . Like a theatre
The rocks had taken curve, as, year by year,
The torrent wore at its hard doom-way, inch by inch . . .
Imagination flew up, then would flinch
From looking down — hung dizzied, even here . . .

We thought: 'God set an awesome gate like this
To cut the low land from the higher land,
As to say: "Now from valley-loveliness,

134

From bounded, sheltering beauty, you are banned.".. .
There are no wooded cliffs above — there cannot be —
   The sky is empty, we can only see
   The severing edge from which the river pours;
   What lies beyond, or be it heaven or hell,
Is not the world we know . . . Yet, truly, who can tell
What, after that last arduous portage, may be ours?
   What sunny plateau covered with new flowers,
   What blest celestial landscape unconfined
To whose blue distances our gleaming way shall wind. . . '

Mind-breath divine (if first such was, alone)
    Element past our ken (if heaven and earth's
Duality from one pure flood be grown)
    Author of your own infinite re-births
        Who in the strife
Of soul with flesh are made known; Way of Truth, of Life

Proved through mortality; supernal word
    Heard but in world-grief; Sun of Righteousness
Who shine but as reluctant evil; Lord
    Incarnate as rebellion, Prince of Peace,
        Emmanuel
Who rule, are with us, through descent to wrath, to Hell,

Your stately names fade as the ancient stars
    That spark our night, whose end is ashes; you
Live on, quickening yet grander, ghostlier wars,
    Kindling fresh holocausts of thought untrue —
        Comfort profane
Is fuel for your marching-fires, again . . . again . . .

AIR & VARIATIONS

AIR & VARIATIONS

1
Nameless for aye,
Our soul's inscrutable sun,
Lord of our ardour's April day,
Doom of our years undone,
You who renew our warm forests from wastes of snow,
You then who leaf them with embers, with ashes, your boon
Of regions, of times is as dust in your temple; this dimly we
                                        know;
We wonder, yet praise not, nor pray.

2
Unsolaced, unstilled
Is our will's revolving sigh,
The world of our circlings unfulfilled
That scan your unmoving sky;
Uncooled is the core of our fierce self-boundaried claim,
Though the breaths of dread beauty, the wafts of a wisdom
                                        too high,
The shine & the cold of your wide ghostly realm have informed
                                        it with shame,
Have created where partly they killed.

3

Your fathomless law
Wherein all that we see,
All that the saints, the prophets saw
Floats like a mote unfree
In beams occult, air-tides invisible,
Your might-through-baffling, your gladness-through-grief
decree,
We meekly acknowledge; we own as our maker your goading
control,
Yet attain but exhaustion & awe;

4

Through leagues of our life
We have fared as a swallow fares,
Who turns from her summer-deserted cliff
And over death's ocean dares,
Whose rest is a rocking of wreckage in fumings of foam,
Or the strain of a mast that points to the tossing stars;
So holds the heart on, whose home is her hope, yet who finds
that her home
Is distance for ever & strife,

5

Till she comes to a place
Unimagined of blaze & calm,
Where stirs even of shore-pillowed ripple no
trace,
No fan-breath of languorous palm,
Where the pinions of thought fall folded, & pain falls tired
As a wind swift-falling, is changed to a nameless balm,
And the isle she desired seems a reef, a resounding no longer
desired,
A blot on the splendour of space . . .

* * *

6

Nor precipice
Of sight nor chasm of sound,
No blinding, deafening gulf was this
That swept so away my ground;
No terror I saw, though rent from the friendly view,
Though severed from voices familiar no sadness I found,
As, freed unawares, my straining attention fell back awhile,
knew
A moment of armistice;

7

The steel-grey guards
Of meaning, the forms I had fought,
Broke rank . . . in a dawn of flowers, of birds,
All night's grim years were naught;
But a sighing held still behind me, my mindful shade,
My shallow earth-image, my anxious, my plodding thought,
That locks in a logic, that folds in old symbols my
glimmerings said:
'What shall I write? What words?'

8

I said: I have seen
The wall of a mountainous wave
Foam into spheres, then sink through green
Of fields to a human grave;
I have followed a sky-filled river, whose flickering throe
Leapt from its actual nodes, to a moon-tide gave
Its might . . . nor forward urge nor backward formed that flow,
Each was the older twin . . .

9

I saw the old dream
Called Being coiled in its urn;
I saw the lids unsealed, the stream
Of dawn-like mist unlearn
Its grasping laws, relive through giving's laws,
Through aimless radiance sombrely discern
The placeless; so did the immense become a cause,
Altered my false extreme;

10

Write this: 'My blind
Earth-wings, my battling brain,
In soul's free sweep, in truth's cool wind
Of ever lessening strain,
In one sunny pulse, whose fall is its forming, whose deed,
Whose rise, is that error's undoing, down-gathered again
To a ground for the same high summons, in this my home-
seeking greed
Feels only *Matter, Mind*.'

*   *   *

11

Unmoved, moving,
Firmament, termless hour,
World's understanding, sky's wide roving,
Past, everlasting power;
Dark womb to whom we life's dark end deny,
Dream-breath whom yet we slay on form's hard floor,
Fount of our blood's low love, hope-cloud whose heaven too
high
Flies from delight's slow proving,

12

Faith-mystery
For ever far, whose gaze
Woos like a brooding soul our sea
Of will's untrodden ways,
Where heave the dim woods of what has not been,
Where dance the unblossomed stars of fresh amaze,
God-light belied, gloom ruling like a sun not seen,
Mocked by no contrary,

13

Shall you, thus rending
As present thought your throne,
Must you not, to man-light's amending,
Seem but his days undone?
Can sombrest freedom be, save in some ray
Of Christly wane? Or must its unreal sun
Resolve, be turned to doomful orbs of night & day,
Be felt as the trouble unending

14

Of worlds that deny
Their plane of linkage, that part
Warm Adam, white Eve with a human sigh,
Heed not creation's heart,
That take for the stream the rocks, the fields, the scene
Of life & death, that of mortal wish & thwart
Make holy war . . . So must it be, so be it. 'Amen'
Is still our creed's blind cry —

15

Pain's dreaded drum,
The call-up of rebel ungrace,
Discharged at last like a child to its home
With the flags of a happy face,
Or flags at dawn, whose day is a ceaseless heaving
Of pride torn down at the close in a cold strange place,
These are gladness, these are labour, these are grieving,
Our birth, our life-tale, our tomb.

*   *   *

16

Not rocky proof
Can lead our lives to bliss;
Thought's tunnelled fort of floor & roof
Ends in a precipice;
Bounded deduction is a wave turned back
That meets its own on-coming — cries 'This, this
Is real' . . . so stands on its original mistake
That should float on, aloof;

17

Not the dead sphere
Of heaven-relation, doomed
To be an island in life's air
Unlimited, entombed
In what it knows not, since its need receives
Only as its own like the leanings gloomed
Of loss, from patient aimless disillusion weaves
Of probing hands a pair;

18

Yet some white coil
Without, red core within,
Must form to make the green world real
That owns no origin;
Though not the imperfect lack can claim a crown
That waits upon its prover, nor can win
To oneness the power-centre, whose impacted sun
Is lack's reciprocal;

19

Your moon, your sun,
Your moved, your moveless power,
Are wills imagined, for the one
Is owned by fleeting hour,
The other stands, & therefore merely seems . . .
How may your time remain, a silver tower?
How your heart-place become unbounded, live, the beams
Of god-light be begun?

20

O truth, move free
From your old mortal stair;
Can you not leave tired certainty
Where it belongs — compare
Knowledge impugned with what may not be known,
That turning, turned, from earth, heaven you declare
Through sacrifice the failure-way that feigns them one . . .
Soul can no further see . . .

*   *   *

146

21

I wrote thus, I wrought
As a castaway sailor must weave
Of spars & brittle rush-rope a boat,
A life-raft whereby he may leave
His island sweet-fruited that holds yet no sweetness of smile;
So twined I my findings, my fortune with will to believe,
So left I the shade-world of glory, was launched from the sad
pleasure-isle,
Knew my past as an earth-point, as naught

22

In the strange, grave sea
Whose powers still unnumbered expand
Like a series of soul to infinity,
With its inverse array no less grand
Of cell within cell (deep needs that for ever descend
As a fraction recurring that finds no last atom) whose
planned
Wave-tides pile outwards & circle within, within, world
without end
For each world of unity . . .

23

Nor lost nor alone
I'll watch the dark's armies awheel;
Though they giddy my thought, though their
calls are unknown
Yet their fellow-commanding I'll feel;
They shall turn in salute with my own slow pole-seeking star,
They shall tremble for truth like my unsleeping needle —
I'll kneel
To a meaning beyond yet within me, too distant to know yet
too near,
To a formless yet fathering throne.

24

For me shall at morn
Smile the flying light-legions; I'll move
To a music serene; beauty newly-born
Shall buoy me, illumed from above;
The grand flow of freedom shall be my guide; now shall be
drowned
Delight's tiny islands, the rock-reefs of limited love,
For the arms everlasting, the seas of earth's leaving, peace
more than profound,
Shall leave me nor weak nor forlorn . . .

*   *   *

25

I wrought thus, I wrote
Me a song, as a wanderer sings
On a storm-torn waste, that inhuman thought
May be stilled, with its vast, vague wings
That rend like a tent his temples . . . a nomad unsure
Is man, now lost in a long night . . . small succour he brings
Who yearns for the earth-hidden sun of some Christ's new
Eden . . . no more
Comes the morn . . . is remembered not . . .

VERSES: SEVENTH BOOK

Can you lay a path
for heart's relieving?
'Yes,' said holy wrath,
'Yes,' said high grieving.

Can you heave a stair
to truth inhuman?
'Yes,' said hope, 'I dare';
said craving: 'I can.'

Can you walk thereon
all day and all night?
'Ah, no,' said undone
love, said altered right.

Can you climb straightly,
never fail, descend?
'Ah, no,' said beauty,
'else should I not be;
heav'n itself would end.'

I saw the daughter of the sun; she stood
Under the north rise of the copse, where now
The shade-hoar faded, where began to show
Pale primrose-heads, fresh as her own pale hood
Of straight hair, groups of early mercury
No greener than her own plain sheeny gown —
Long had I wandered in the winter-town
Of smoke-grey fog, of stone-grey field and tree.

Nor girl she seemed, nor goddess; her grave face,
Soft as a child's, yet wise, brighter than spring,
More warm than summer, had strange shadowing,
Than mundane lustre held both more and less;

No mirth was there, no glee, no eagerness,
No love, save love for every living thing.

Heart nor proud nor pined,
heart that leaves behind
honours, reverses,
that like summer breeze
goes its way, is blind

to the worldly scene
of withered or green,
vineyard or graveyard,
that moves without word
like a pensive queen

on its path apart
of warm high purport —
earth is your kingdom,
heaven is your home,
lonely, sunny heart.

3
The Acacia

Not yet, nor soon,
My still delaying, still unflowering tree,
Shall you create, set free
Your quiet lights, your smiles at sun and moon.

Toil's ready bough
Is strong; shall it not bear, make real what still
Comes but to shams of skill,
To sterile shine of breeze-turned leaves? — Ah, no,

My too slow tree,
Still unredeemed is your laborious year . . .
I know what soulless fear
It is that chills you, blights what you should be.

4

He said: The city is a forest; look, out there,
At all the branchy signal-trees — oaks in the glade
Of the great junction, at those pines, twigless and spare,
The chimneys of the factory, that hold their shade
(Their glooms of smoke) up so aloofly, crossed by these
Frail crowding vines of wire that droop from bole to bole;
Or listen to the busy hustling of the breeze —
Of ceaseless traffic, of the streets' entangled soul.

He said: Nature who built the sunny vista-ways
Of the green forest made our sombre forest too —
She who creates our groves as well of inward gaze
Throughout the ages, timbering thickly thought's small view,

Rearing more starkly, tensely, beauty's slow-taught forms,
Wakening our winds of zeal, even our disastrous storms.

5
Jerusalem, September 17, 1948

Olive-gloomed city of earth's grave shaming,
white-towered city, too, of our shining pride;
foul city, that cast out, that slew a King,
fair city, home of Hero deified;
city whose sombre-lawed stark religion's
black-flint angers it was that first struck fire
from brighter law — that woke with its brute stones
the angel-steel of love's well-tempered ire,

now are our hearts yet again your tinder,
kindled, ravaged once more by pride, by shame;
man's elements, we see, are as they were
two thousand years ago, their strife the same;

now to truth's old feud you add another
clash — of wrath, mercy locked in mortal flame.

To the stars I sighed:
'Must you keep your crown,
be still panoplied
in silence, in frown?'
They answered: 'Our glow
is your thought's own throe.'

To the surging woods
to the wave-green plains,
I murmured: 'Doom broods
in your shifty fanes.'
They said: 'Your own sea,
your wild soul, are we.'

Then on man I turned
eyes tear-reddened, cheek
with anger that burned,
lips that burned to speak;
but the cold world cried
'Your own heart I hide.'

Dutiful volunteer, who yesterday
Vowed to a flag your ardours infinite,
Now that you are released examine it;
Look at the slanted crosses first and say:
'This white, this almost over-ridden one,
Is what my rival asks of landed might;
And this thin red one is my neighbour's right,
The ground where endless quarrels are begun;

But this broad upright one, above the rest,
The reaching arms, the cross of him who killed
The dragon, this stands for the threatened field
Of my own grasp — is mercy's faith professed

By mortal fear' . . . Go, thank God on your knees
For peace, you whose war-thoughts are only these.

Prisoner, in whose tired bearing still I read
The martial canons of uprightness, pride,
The quiet rules of your too-sounding creed,
Of soaring grasp that your resolve should guide;
In whose wan visage plainly still appear
Marks of the muses' rarer, subtler writ,
Of law melodious that aloft can bear
The mind imperial that has mastered it;

You rode the wind, who tranquil take your fall.
Checked by the fences of terrestrial fate,
Brought up short suddenly by the blank wall,
Calmly your regal thought you dedicate

To this — that grudgingly dull earth may state:
He died with dignity. This is your all.

Once in winter grey
on a field of snow
at fading of day
when the wind was low,

sighed on my white thought
what that world had been,
what dawns had made what
mists of April green,

what high thunder-noons
strewn what colours bold,
what chill, grave evens
given what tender gold . . .

Then the bent old sun,
low in deathly haze,
said: 'My sceptre, crown
and orb are undone . . .
take my broken throne' —
broke me with his gaze . . .

A glare-lit wall-cliff; windows row on row
Glare-lit, too, from within; at each a face —
Three, four dazed faces — looking down, down . . . space
Is drawn out here; time pauses, crawls, slow, slow . . .
Those tiny too-short wisps of white, I know,
Are knotted sheets . . . Where is the reaching grace
Of fire-chute, ladder? . . . O delayed help, race
Rashlier . . . madly! . . . The picture passes . . . O

But how roused feeling follows it . . . first soars
To those high furnace-traps, with terror sees
The street's abyss . . . flies down then, stands afreeze
With powerless pity; then leaps hours, explores

In chill of dawn, rooms charred, sky-roofed, where mind
Stumbles, a stranger, fears what it may find.

This is the last night that my love is here;
I will not sleep, I'll sit beside my dear,

Watching the worn face that I know so well,
Staring the thoughts out that no words can tell.

He does not speak, he gives no sign; the room
Familiar chills me, is no more a home.

Tomorrow we shall ride away, not side
By side now, but apart, like groom and bride

To church, to start another life; yes, there
I'll lose my being, alter into air,

Watch, far away, a woman stand or kneel,
Hear, absently, her voice of muffled steel,

Then, after, see her slowly turn, go back,
Unlock the door, take off her new-bought black,

And set about to do what must be done
In the still house where she now lives alone . . .

This is the last night that my love is here;
He sees me not; I sit and dumbly stare.

12
For —

He said: I left it in the porch, my wreath of rue,
      And went in; there the staid
Prayers met me kindly, the majestic music drew
      Me close, had arms to aid;

The blessing was a hand's warm grasp; but when once more
      I stepped out in the sun
(He said) the whispering elms, the look the daisies wore
      Had me again undone,

And all the eager crowds of April jostled me,
      Went their own way (he said)
Whose business is not with the past, who brutally
      Deal no more with the dead.

There are floods that feed
each field in season;
when their task is done
orderly recede;

there are floods whose new
course of scouring rage
works awhile damage;
and floods are there, too,

that turn the rich plain
into mire and wrack,
whose folk come not back,
on whose brackish track
spring shall plant in vain.

What you sigh for, that will you receive —
this is the punishment from which there's no reprieve.

What you cry to, that will you become —
this is creation's law, life's dread, most certain doom.

Fear not, what you shun will not be yours —
squand'ring of comfort, strength, its sale for unseen stores;

What you blame, despise, you'll never be —
pauper, vagrant — no, nor prophet, divinity.

Old hunter for youth's head,
    These are your old decoys —
A matron diamonded,
    A man with golden toys;

And these, too, long ago,
    Were children that you charmed —
This lad who failed to grow,
    This girl still empty-armed.

Moored in the shallows, clogged with barnacle,
Her tackle gone, the stately galleon lies,
A hulk, yet trimly painted, serving still
The need of reverent or of curious eyes;
She who was powered once by supernal airs
Now in the lee of a huge liner's hull —
A blank grey engine-wall — unmoving wears
Her strange prow-mask, her carvings fanciful.

She is no longer seaworthy; her crew,
The sons of simple fishers, long are dead;
Even to tell her tale remain but few —
To sing the days when, Europe's hope or dread,

Her sails were clouds, her mast a lighting-rod
From heaven to earth — her name, *The Glory of God* .

17
The Railroad

Along the iron rails
Plod still with panting power,
Range still the empty trails
  Hour after hour;

Stare still where looms ahead
Each signal-skeleton,
Whose jerking arms forbid
  Or bid you on,

Whose grim lamps rule the glooms
With stringent red or green —
Forget your sunny home's
  Wild-paths between

Primrose and violet,
Your breeze-lit fields of rye . . .
Your golden sheaves forget —
  Forget, or die.

Either of these you are, too mindful soul;
Or earth's firm self, a final singular,
Based on your pale collective's broken shoal,
Then on abstraction, wreck of sense and star;
Or, proof forswearing, an adventurous wave,
You found induction on the sun you feel,
Dismiss your glory-moon, yourself a slave
Squander in circling service all your zeal.

Either — no, both and neither . . . At the best,
Throned as a ghost that has no more to give,
You find on your imagined height no rest,
Only again the same alternative,

Another *Time or Place*, a fateful stair
Between a heaven's *Not yet*, a world's *Not here*.

19

Sweet Humility,
Wound, awaken me;

Smite my too high head
With your loftier dread;

Pierce my wild-winged heart
With your truth's far dart;

Rend my soul too grand
With wide grieving, and,

When all this is done,
When I'm crushed, unmanned,
Heal me, happy one.

Doomed sun, who to yourself so tensely draw
The flying planets of your phantom past,
Who own no light but the old blind-writ law
Of moveless proof, of force's myth made fast;
Hard heart of grasping stress, who still deny
That airier stress through whom alone you are,
The radiance without whose brave loss you die,
The timeless breath of your time-bodied star,

Turn, be uncrowned, alter your cause, your creed;
Rush out, look elsewhere; win to suffering's ways;
Consume your power's dark path; be power indeed;
Undo pride; for the orbs of former days

Are dust; only their sacrificial beams,
Their unfulfilled are, so, unending dreams.

Get thee behind me, Satan . . . like a sun I stood . . .
　　　　　My burning mood
Made earth a desert, bred more serpents unsubdued.

Get thee behind me . . . like a storm I fought . . . Hell's sea
　　　　　Hurled up to me
Its wrecking floods the faster . . . then, despairingly,

I turned, took up my humble human spade and hoe,
　　　　　Laboured, and lo,
The world seemed Eden, as it was long years ago.

Not strife is life, I know, not anxiousness,
Not endless need but loss for ever new;
Not stubborn thunder-towers of thwarted stress,
But morning mist redeemed as evening dew;
Not smiting light mocked by its tropic sand,
But light dissolved in pomp of temperate seas,
Or turned to wonders on a wintry land,
To purple, gold, of ghostlier panoplies.

It is not torrent, but a stream that flows
Through grass, through garden, with ecstatic songs;
It is the ray that's lost in leaf and rose,
Whose glory never to itself belongs;

It is the grace in air, in smile; it grieves
At no forgoing; gives blindly, believes.

This I'll do, nor deem
    My soul unsuited —
Grudge to none my gleam
    Of pearl transmuted,

Keep no crystal back
    Of eyes' clear lighting,
Let no sapphire lack
    Its flashed requiting,

Grant to each heart-wound
    My ruby grieving,
Lend my diamond
    For mind's relieving . . .

So I'll wane, yet say
    I've lost no jewel,
For my names are *Nay,*
    Not here, Renewal.

There is no truth, only the proof's arraigning;
There is no life, only delight's refraining;

There is no doom, only the truth's enchaining;
There is no lie, only delight's retaining;

Says the fresh wind above the world of feigning:
'I am not mortal, who have no remaining.'

When from beside you
on the dais goes
all that your soul chose,

when, one after one,
from the hall are gone
all your mind-loves too,

and the helpers rest
from their to and fro,
have slipped from the feast;

when wine is no more,
when the lights burn low,
when the windy door

is set wide open,
stand up, you, to go;
like a master, then,
make your exit slow.

For a Mathematician

I asked: What, then, is power? You said: Within
A power whose name is *Naught* (a waveless sea
Of ground and progress) must far back begin
The meson-points of possibility —
Infinitesimals that swell to founts
Of sum material, in whose body blind
Moves then the logarithmic pulse that mounts,
Three-fold at last, to birth of different mind.

Nor river-raft, nor scudding tidal sail
(Nor simple drift nor drift factorial)
Is this free hull, whose engine cannot fail
Its own direction, that within its wall

Turns to identity each unseen hour
Of past's repudiation . . . This is Power . . .

Power is not this: a pulse of *whence* and *when*,
Of wills disparate, waned to seem a pair;
Mind's one assumption, earth's implied *Amen*,
Atom and cosmos locked in throbbing air;
Nor this: alternativity's knit throe
Of life whose might is blind, yet timeless, vast,
And tiny helpless life that yet can know;
These, a low need, are power's imagined past.

Power is what says this moment, here, in me:
'My ardent self, my earth-life, is not I —
Is but the passion-ground whence poesy
Hurls itself calmly to a half-seen sky

Whose light unformed leads me to spend, to spend
My fiery world of form, world without end.'

M

A summit-field it was, moor-grass that met
Unhindered airs, an open hermitage,
A very world-roof, with its parapet
Of ocean-blue, and on that lonely stage
A birch was dancing; like a soul apart
Had lost her earth-life to a lord unseen,
Knew only fervour, praised through mindless art
Of white limbs waving, skirts of swirling green.

The noon-breeze was her music; warm, full wind,
Swaying this way and that her ready form,
Fashioned her frenzy, drove her strifes to find
Strifes ever wider, was her fond will-storm

That told of foam's white boughs, of verdurous seas,
Of grace more grand yet, of celestial trees.

29

Three lifts below him
link him with the void;
three above, though dim,
keep his spirit buoyed;

forms opposed, so paired
to fix him a place
between fog-hazard
and truth's hidden face;

arms that hold him — reach
from he knows not where;
wings that he must stretch,
himself, into air;

arms of groundless proof,
wings of proof unsure,
between a dream-roof
and a hollow floor . . .

What are plume and limb
to touch heaven and hell?
What is the world's rim? . . .
Ask *him* . . . ask *him* . . .
who but he can tell . . .

If there's no ruling,
only lot's empire,
what is sorrow's lyre?
Why should danger sing?

Why should poverty
be a fluted stream?
Why should trouble seem
the drums, the glory-

fifes of ocean-shows? —
Why should the world ring,
if time has no string
of rightful tuning,
only random blows?

Once trouble wove
With doom a wildwood beauty, fastened down
Her boughs of action grand,
Gripped like a pine's her senses' trembling crown,
Twined with a lifeless strand
Her very sighing — meshed her that she might not move,

And like a pine's
Becalmed arms, so too her grave inward sway
Grief tightened, the true lines
Knit tenselier of her needled thought, as where
Warm wingy hopes had seemed
Like singing hues, now only a grey wood-dove dreamed.

No rash spring air,
No wrath's familiar equinoctial fray
Was this still thunder-hold
That to her human times the flash foretold —
This slow word that did weave
Her life with loss; made her, so, readier to receive.

Song

When dour winter is undone,
Slain the lord of revelry,
When the glowing pomps are gone
Of tall summer's tenancy,
When frail autumn's lonely throne
Crumbles like a frosted stone,

When the stars' white sands are run,
Quenched the orbs of woe and glee,
When the brazen lamp's o'erthrown
And the lamp of ivory,
Then, O, then are you begun,
Season of a ghostlier sun.

What is it to love? It is to be torn
with fear lest your strong Love leave you forlorn;
it is to tremble every time you see
your delicate Love, lest suddenly she
shall fail and leave you comfortless . . . But *I*
am a lover whose Love can never die.

Frenzying love is to dread lest you lose
some sheltering arm, to shrink from, to refuse
the hand of wintry Sacrifice . . . but I
call *him* my lord, my life . . . who also cry,
caressed with summer-wealth, with bliss too free:
'Fair Calm, you kill ev'n as you comfort me.'

These are the briefs of being, by being scanned:
First, the vast cause, slandered infinity,
Where points of minor time dark proof expand
Of light's own speed, of ether; secondly
The argument where clues of cosmic stress
Weave to a scheme of rigid worlds that run
To life-conclusion; then the intense address
Called thought soars, dwells on its own heights outdone,

And, last of mights imagined, cries: 'No more
Let fire rely on some far fallacy;
No longer is light's axiom now secure —
The blank reflection of my baffled plea. . .'

Reformulates all being on formless base;
Comes, so, to briefs unseen, to spirit's case.

How on solemn fields of space
Black with amplitude sublime
Form the starry flowers of time;

How the centuries replace
Lifeless worlds with worlds of green,
Scenes of rock with forest scene;

How the city, proud yet mean,
For whose sake a wildwood burned
In its turn at last despairs,

Falls before the horde of years,
All this is but thought returned,
This that we have fixed we find . . .

Till on proof by proof destroyed,
On the waste-mounds of the mind,
Soul's vague lily scents the void.

36
Song

Clear it away, all
that's low, unthinking;
keep but the final
might of mind, the king;

strength is but a tool,
eager, flickering eye
only a candle
lit to labour by,

and heart a measure
that wrongly rules: 'This,
that *I* mark, is sure,
all else is amiss.' . . .

Fierce is thought's refrain,
but the lover knows
that language is vain —
grace in silence goes.

37
For P. W.

Nor field nor garden — nor the wilful growth
Of utter wildness nor the mannered grace
Of formal husbandry; what once was chase
Unkempt, he of whom tell I, nothing loth
To image in his home his happy mind,
Turned first to even grass, then cut free-hand
The winding beds, massed there a wealth unplanned
Of all earth's flowers, the fairest he could find.

Yet still, moulding the smooth lawn, you may see
The wold's weak hollows and strong-grounded swell
Scarce altered; and he, too, of whom I tell,
Gentle, a full-crowded epitome

Of culture, yet keeps his loved gifts and flaws
As God made them, unlevelled by man's laws.

Strew beauty everywhere; all tombs are one;
strew it in the catacombs of lost delight,
strew wreaths of sweetness, smiles that need no more the sun.

Strew it on the crumbling earth-mounds of might;
strew it on the low graves of shame; strew it on
the sodden cemeteries of nor wrong nor right.

Have you withheld from vaulty wrath one rose?
Have you ever denied to lightless desire
one lily-glance, some balm of brightness? Has what glows

now only on the past's avoided pyre
wrought you at last a doom more dire ev'n than those
of cold, of dark — turned memory's embers to fire?

Dedication for a Book of Poems

For one I'll name not
limned I such an one;
of her world I wrote,
spoke so my passion;

I thought: 'Her courage
on this wave will ride;
her heart's anchorage
will accept this tide;'

I drew a cloudscape
for her mind's high land —
meant: 'Surely, this shape,
this, she'll understand,

and this tall forest
(I sighed) she'll extol,
sighing: "I can rest
here, at will, my soul" . . . '

And recked I never
of earth's boundary —
too late I limned her
woods, and sky, and sea.

Sorrow and care, who dog me now by night, by day,
Marring my rest with your old yarns of misery,
Of what's past mending, or of what may never be,
Of long agos discoloured, of a future grey;
You, the decrepit ne'er-do-weel who hour on hour
Fumble the ragged bandage of some ancient sore,
And you, whose lean hag-face is lined with omen-lore —
Drear hangers-on, low haunters of life's every tower,

Since you'll not leave me, this at least I'll drive you to —
Work for my betterment; this shall *you* do for me:
Widen in time my window; batter till I see
Further than formerly down some sad street; and *you*

Weave me at last a flag that anxious eyes may bless —
An ensign of warm aid, of white unworldliness.

There's a path, as I suppose,
From the bee-mouth to the rose,
Or no garden were, no hive;

There's a guide, as I can guess,
For the feet of eagerness,
Where the jungle comes alive.

There's a way, as I know well,
That no bee, no beast can tell,
That nor scented is nor seen,

Till the sudden envoy dares,
Till the flying smile declares:
'I am bright where love has been.'

This (I said) *is mine:*
to rule my willing:
yet my ruling's line
is an ended ring,

for my passion, fear,
are a written page;
how can I alter
my heart-heritage?

If I change my loves
I must be other;
I must be what moves
here and yet not here,

a valiant spiral
reaching to the void,
to the strange, my wall,
to my will, destroyed . . .

Only what is not
can be true, remain,
false is the pivot
of the factual brain,

the blank imagined
by bewildered thought,
an eye-mist where mind
sees its least as Naught;

or, soaring midnight
sits with blinding sun;
or, lofty delight
with delight undone,

or, glorious battle
is the dark's low king;
or, a lord of all
feels our suffering . . .

This is deity,
this endures, is truth,
in one heaven to see
rage's height and ruth,

to exalt as one
certainty, despair,
to forge the same crown
for foul and for fair,

in your church of clay,
at last, side by side,
cold as stone to lay
body and his bride . . .

Ay, for the high cause
of our task intense
lives but in his laws,
is not *here* but *hence* . . .

What are you, dark boat,
tiny moving blot
on a wide vague sea?
'I am *Here, now* — pause
between *Nowhere was*
and *Never can be*.'

How could *Is* from *Naught*
arise, and what wrought
your link, your pattern?
'My small floating dock
forms my floating rock,
the rafts at my stern.'

What are you, calm wave,
or support, or grave,
or thrust, or limit?
'I am not, nor die;
my bond, passing by,
lives on, incomplete.'

What then, placeless king,
can house you, hurling
homes away, make known
what is not? . . . 'You, you,
small thought-ship untrue,
tiny human throne.'

Fathomless, too free,
    Unpowered, unrooted,
How may Unity
    Create, be fruited?

Through the mortal stem
    Of man's remaining;
By the stratagem
    Of grandeur's feigning.

How may boundless might's
    Nor gain nor losing
Touch those tiny heights
    Of fate's refusing?

When the wintry dream
    Stirs as a dreamer,
Then may dying seem
    Its own redeemer,

Then may truth be known
    In wrecks of lying,
Heaven itself look down
    As self-denying.

The whitening villages, the down
   Now hueless under dusty snow,
The hedges half-erased, the brown
   Farm-written tracks of to and fro,

The broken threads of lane and brook,
   The parchment of discoloured sky,
These are the cover of a book
   That shall be opened, by and by.

These are old winter's wrapping worn,
   The title of its vacant days;
Within is writ the biding corn,
   Are limned a myriad hearths ablaze.

One said (no dream
it was, but real day)
'Sigh not, though I seem
    absent, nor say

that you no more
can touch, hear, see me —
think not your labour
    solitary.

Mine are your hands,
through my eyes you gaze
at the undug lands
    of future days;

your inward ears
hear the same lord's voice,
the endless orders
    (sigh not rejoice)

that I heard too,
O my groping child' —
this he said, then through
    my lips he smiled.

47

The Birchwood
(For C. G. N. his water-colour)

    Further than this
(You say) *none go* . . . Deep in a wintry wood
I seem of birch; a skyless, blind abyss
    Of white boughs that have strewed

    Or still uphold
Their flaming haze; one only line of black
There is, that runs from golden mist to misty gold,
    A pine-log, the straight track

    Bridging some stream
Or bog or chasm too ghostly still to see;
Only this road-span, in a land of dream
    Lives, is reality.